Kirsty Logan's books incl ....
in the Dark, The Gloamin, ...
and The Rental Heart & Other Fairytales ... ...
with her wife, baby and rescue dog.

'I loved *The Unfamiliar* – a courageous and sharply written account of a meandering journey to motherhood and all the emotional and physical struggles it entails. Funny and intensely moving, with the most vivid description of birth I've ever read' Kate Maxwell, author of *Hush*

'Cold, hard, raw writing that somehow sets your heart on fire. I could not put it down' Laura Dockrill, author of *What Have I Done?*

'Searingly honest. There is something inherently strange about nurturing a person inside your body and then giving birth to it ... Logan does an excellent job of portraying the reality – the beauty and the horror of it' Lotte Jeffs, *Guardian*

'Logan manages to bring the tiniest detail in kaleidoscopic detail for the reader, but in such precise poetic prose' Pragya Agarwal, author of *(M)otherhood*

'Kirsty Logan writes with bright wit and wonder – I read this book in awe' Doireann Ní Ghríofa, author of *A Ghost in the Throat*

The Unfamiliar

A Queer Motherhood Memoir

Kirsty Logan

virago

VIRAGO

First published in Great Britain in 2023 by Virago
This paperback edition published in Great Britain in 2024 by Virago

3 5 7 9 10 8 6 4 2

Copyright © Kirsty Logan 2023

The moral right of the author has been asserted.

*Some details have been changed to protect the identities of the donors.
We're hugely grateful to both our donors, who gave us a generous and
life-changing gift. I would encourage anyone who is physically and
emotionally able to consider the possibility of sperm donation.*

A CIP catalogue record for this book
is available from the British Library.

ISBN 978-0-349-01658-0

Typeset in Garamond by M Rules
Printed and bound in Great Britain by
Clays Ltd, Elcograf S.p.A.

Papers used by Virago are from well-managed forests
and other responsible sources.

Virago
An imprint of
Little, Brown Book Group
Carmelite House
50 Victoria Embankment
London EC4Y 0DZ

An Hachette UK Company
www.hachette.co.uk

www.virago.co.uk

To our babies,
the one who made it
and the ones who didn't

'Some days it feels like writing truthfully about her own life is the most subversive thing a woman can do.'

JENN ASHWORTH

'There is only a queer, divine dissatisfaction, a blessed unrest...'

MARTHA GRAHAM, as quoted in *Martha: The Life and Work of Martha Graham* by AGNES DE MILLE

The Planning

The Planning

1

You and your partner want a baby. But your two bodies can't make a baby together. So you need some sperm.

You have some friends who would make good donors. One says no because he might want his own kids some day. One says yes, then later no because you won't be raising the baby in his religion. One says no because he might be moving abroad soon. You don't mind them saying no; better that than saying yes and backing out later, or worse – saying yes, a baby coming, and then regretting it.

But still. Every time you hear *no*, it's harder to respond with, *Totally fine! Thanks for even considering it! We'll ask*

another of the rapidly dwindling pool of people we know who
have sperm and might give us some! :) xx

If you had sperm and you weren't using it, would you give it
to someone? You're not sure. You have lots of things you're
not using that you don't want to give away. Some of these
things in your body, some in your home, and some not
tangible things at all, like your time or your attention. You
have them and other people need them. But still. They're
yours, aren't they? You don't owe them to anyone. You can
keep them all to yourself if you want.

And if you're honest, you do. You luxuriate, like a dragon
on its hoard, on the shining piles of your time and your
attention, knowing that there are people out there who
could use them. People who have babies but do not have
sufficient time or attention. Couldn't you share yours
with them?

But they already have a baby.

But you're not entitled to a baby. You're not entitled to
anyone's sperm.

You and your partner go out for dinner. You order a soft-
shell crab burger, thinking it will be a patty, minced, in
breadcrumbs. It's an entire deep-fried crab in a bun, which

looks exactly like a spider. Its legs stick out of the side. You don't dare open the bun because you're afraid to see if it has eyes. You try to eat it fast but only manage half. You have stomach ache for hours, so bad that you force yourself not to cry out. You don't admit that you didn't like your dinner or that you're in pain. That night you dream you give birth to a hundred tiny crabs, scuttling out of your body and across the crumpled sheets.

You and your partner quickly exhaust your potential sperm donor list. It wasn't that long; you don't know that many people with sperm, mostly the boyfriends or husbands of your female friends. And they mostly want the sperm for themselves.

You don't even like sperm. Or rather semen. You always hated it. Even in the years that you were still fucking men, the semen was your least favourite part. The bleachy smell of it. The tapioca texture. The way it dried on your skin, making it sticky and grubby-feeling. You got it out of you, off of you, as quickly as you could. You liked fucking men, but the sperm you could have done without. You remember reading a character in a novel who had no testicles, only a penis, and thinking: Oh, perfect.

And now look at you. Politely asking your every acquaintance for some sperm, pretty please.

After the last *no*, the one from the friend who wanted the baby raised in his religion, which isn't even your religion, which is none, or your partner's religion, which is lapsed, you despair. You despair dramatically, cinematically, flopping on the couch and weeping into the cushions. *It's not fair*, you wail to your partner, like a toddler. *It's not fair*.

Even as you write this you think: Why are you mocking yourself? Because you remember crying on that couch. You remember the ache, the disappointment, the devastation you felt at being told, once again, that you weren't going to have a baby. Weren't even going to get the chance to try. Other people can have babies. They can have babies when they don't even mean to. But not you.

Because it wasn't just sperm, was it? You're using the word sperm over and over and it's kind of funny, it's a funny word, it makes people titter and blush. But every *no* isn't the loss of some sperm. It's the loss of a child you hoped you could have with your partner. It's the loss of a life you are desperately trying to build together.

You and your partner mourn the loss of every one of those babies you'd hoped for. With each person you asked, you couldn't help studying their faces. The texture of their hair. The angle of their jaw. The subtle catch of their tongue on their bottom teeth. Mixing these features with the more familiar ones you see every day, thinking: Is this what our child will look like? Is this our future?

You want to keep wailing and weeping on the couch, but your partner immediately goes online and finds a website. The website is like internet dating, but for sperm. People who have sperm and are willing to give it away put up profiles with their location, life situation and photo. People who need sperm put up similar profiles. *Let's just look*, she says.

You met your partner online. Later you both admitted that you didn't like one another's photos – she didn't like the fake-fur coat you were wearing, thinking it meant you were high-maintenance and princessy; you didn't like the beanie hat she was wearing, thinking it meant she was young and immature and probably still skateboarded. But you gave one another a chance and went for a drink anyway. It turned out she was actually four years older than you and had never skateboarded in her life. You, however, can't deny being high-maintenance.

She says she knew you were the one as soon as you walked into the bar. For you it took a little longer; after drinks you went to dinner, and when she ordered ox cheek she paused, grinned, and pinched her own cheek. That's when you knew.

You stayed in that restaurant, like the old cliché, until the staff were sweeping up around your feet. Your partner, tipsy and giddy, already in love, already knowing she was sitting across from her future, tipped so much that the waiter returned the notes, thinking it was a mistake. At the taxi rank she asked to kiss you, and you said yes, and she slipped her hands inside that fake-fur coat that you didn't know she didn't like, and you whispered into her mouth: *Can I come home with you?* And she replied: *No, next time. I want it to last.*

You browse the sperm donor website together. It lists three different methods for donation: IVF, home insemination using cups and syringes, or 'natural conception', which is a euphemism for penetrative sex, and which you will only refer to in inverted commas because it seems to you deeply unnatural to fuck someone you don't want to fuck purely to get sperm. You avoid every profile that lists 'natural conception' as the only option, which it turns out is a depressingly high number.

You see a queer person you vaguely know, a friend-of-a-friend-of-a-friend who you've spoken to at literary events. They seemed fine, if a little socially awkward. But you're shocked to see that they've listed 'natural conception' as their only option. You think it would be nice to have a fellow queer person as your donor. But not that one.

You and your partner make a profile on the sperm donor website with several photos of you together, smiling, looking wholesome. You hope you don't seem princessy or skateboardy, or if you do, the potential donors don't mind. You include a photo of you both with your dog, a lurcher you adopted together several years ago, and who has taught you many things that you hope will be useful for parenthood, like patience and loving discipline and night-waking and observing the health and wellbeing of a creature that can't tell you if something hurts and cleaning up shit and pee and puke and generally keeping alive something other than yourself.

You also include a photo from your wedding, an event you planned because you loved each other and wanted to show your commitment and quite fancied a big party with your family and friends. But, honestly, it was mostly so that you'd both be legal parents to the baby you'd already agreed you both wanted, something you discussed on the third date, which seems funny to you now, a queer cliché, a red flag even, but at the time seemed perfectly logical; you already knew you were going to be together so it made sense to get the details sorted. If you weren't married at the time of conception, then the non-birth parent wouldn't automatically be the baby's other parent, and would have to wait and adopt the baby after the birth. It would also mean you'd have to write the sperm donor's name on the birth certificate, as it's illegal not to name the 'father' if you know who it is. Neither of you wanted that. So you're married, and you'll both automatically be the parents of the baby you conceive together. You don't want to be heterosexual, and never have. You don't think you should have had to get married just to be equal parents. But you did it. To get what straight people have, sometimes you have to play by the rules they made.

You find a donor. He says he's studying to be a physiotherapist, he's from the Highlands, he spends a lot of time with his nephews. He also says he's healthy and has had a full STD check. You have no proof of this, but have to trust him. He's already fathered six other children for six different women; though he doesn't call this fathering, he calls it helping, as in, *I've helped six women*. You don't know if you've ever been more grateful for someone's help in your life.

Things you and your partner ask the donor:

- Any family health problems?

- Do these fertile dates work with your schedule?

- Can we cover your travel costs?

Things you want to ask the donor:

- Does it make you feel manly to father lots of children?

- Do you find it sexy when women are pregnant by you?

- Do you bring specific porn for when you masturbate in strangers' bathrooms? What is it?

He comes to your flat and he's young, shy. Your partner has popped to the shop to get some biscuits, so you invite the donor in and offer him tea, coffee, juice, water. He doesn't want anything. He sits in the furthest-away chair, tucked in the corner. You chat awkwardly for a while. You don't know what's the appropriate length of time to chat to him. The thing is that he's not your friend. You've never met him before and to be honest you're not particularly interested in him as a person. But you don't want him to know that. You don't want him to feel used, like you're only interested in him for his sperm, even though you are quite literally only interested in his sperm.

Your partner returns with the entire biscuit section of the supermarket. The donor says he doesn't want a biscuit, thank you. You're relieved that she's back; you know she's more likeable than you, funnier and more casual; you know you come across as stuck-up and distant when you're nervous. More than anything, you want the donor to like you. You want him to feel you're worthy of what he's giving you.

Eventually there's an extended pause and he says, *Should we . . . ?* And so you do. Your donor goes into your bathroom to masturbate. Your partner goes into the bedroom to masturbate. You stay on the couch, not masturbating. You put the TV on. The flat is small and quiet, and you don't want them to feel like you can hear their intimate sounds. You don't want them to be able to hear each other. Or would that help him? Does he find the whole thing strangely arousing, or is it a mere physical chore, like cutting his toenails?

Your partner wants to orgasm both before and after the semen goes in. She's read that the rhythmic pulses of an orgasm will pull the semen up into the womb and help with conception. This seems frankly ludicrous to you, but then again this whole thing feels ludicrous.

You fidget on the couch. How long is it supposed to take? You turn the TV volume down. You don't want to distract either of them with inappropriate and unsexy sounds. The choice is *Countdown* or *Judge Judy* (but who could orgasm to the ticking clock or the bang of the gavel?).

Sexy TV would be even worse. This isn't sexy. This isn't sex. But both of them need to orgasm, separately, in separate rooms, without thinking about what each other is doing. And you need to sit here and pretend you're watching TV and not waiting for two orgasms.

You hear the bathroom lock click. You feel it would cheapen the whole thing to offer him money, but you want to offer him something. You can't think what, so you just thank him when he leaves the little tub of semen on your toilet tank, hoping he can see from your shining, wide-open eyes how genuine you are.

You carry the semen through to the bedroom tucked in your bra to keep it at body temperature. Your partner is on the bed, naked from the waist down, lower body propped on pillows. She's masturbating, eyes closed, focused. You lurk by the door. You can smell her cunt. It's arousing.

I could help, you'd said to your partner the night before. You'd imagined candles, music, kissing; a coming together. You'd imagined a sex act, the way most babies are conceived. Well, not exactly the same way. You know how to make her come; you've done it a lot. You've done it seven times in one session. That was in the early days of your relationship, but even several years in you're a reliable provider of between one and three orgasms a time. *We could do it together*, you say. *No*, your partner replies, then softens. *It's not about you. I don't find it sexy to have a random man's bodily fluids in me. We just have to get it done.*

You'd imagined fucking like you usually fuck. But this isn't fucking. This is a physical chore, like cutting your toenails.

Except when your partner cuts her toenails, she doesn't have her legs spread, and her cunt wet, and her labia swollen and pink, and she's not making the orgasm sounds you know so well.

You stand by the door, a tub of stranger's semen in your bra, a throbbing between your legs. Your body is confused. Your partner orgasms, you put the semen in the syringe, you squirt it into her cunt, she orgasms again, she rests her legs straight up the wall, you go and make cups of tea, and while the kettle boils you think: maybe that was it, maybe she's pregnant, maybe that will be the story that you laughingly, wonderingly tell people about how you made a baby together. The kettle clicks off. The flat smells of sex.

Your donor comes every month. But every month, so does your partner's period.

2

You take part in a performance night in an abandoned theatre. You read your story while lying in an empty bath, wearing a white dress, your face painted white. You've had a glass of wine and you worry it has stained your lips; the night was badly organised and you didn't have time to look in the mirror before going on stage. Afterwards your friend shows everyone her new puppy, which is very tiny, about the size of a four-month-old foetus. She hands you the dog and you hold it tenderly, cooing over how tiny it is. There doesn't seem to be much else to say about the dog other than its size.

You feel a sudden urge to throw the dog at the wall. Just fling it with all your strength. It's the same compulsion you get to open the car door on the motorway, or post your wallet into a postbox, or chuck your phone off a bridge into the river. You read once that this is called the imp of the perverse, and that it's just your brain reminding itself what it's not supposed to do. You don't think you will actually throw the dog. But still you hand the dog to your partner, saying, *Look how small!*

Later, on the long midnight drive home, you confess to your partner about the urge to throw the dog. *Me too!* she says. *But you didn't throw it*, you say. *Neither did you*, she replies.

On the sixth try, you achieve a new closeness with your donor when he confesses that he has a website of photos he's taken of different wood grains. You already know this, as well as his hometown and parents' names and place of work, because you've thoroughly internet-stalked him. But you express surprise and admiration anyway. You want to ask him about wood grains, to show that you're interested in him beyond his sperm, which you're actually not, but you can't think of anything to ask.

While he's masturbating in your bathroom, you google 'unusual wood grains'. You find an Etsy shop that sells a variety of decorative silver items carved with genuine wood grain patterns. You save several of the items, thinking that to show your donor appreciation for all he's done, you'll get one of them as a gift when a baby is finally, inevitably born.

Your body is no longer confused by your partner masturbating. You wait patiently by the door with the cup of semen in your bra. You stay quiet so you don't distract her. You don't feel aroused. She orgasms quickly and efficiently. You go to make tea.

You and your partner don't fuck during the two-week wait before it's possible to do a pregnancy test, because if she is pregnant then the orgasm or the fucking could cause a problem. You don't in the week after the pregnancy test either, because it's always negative and you're both too sad. The slim window between is when you can come together, a time for lying naked together and kissing and touching and licking and fucking, and for orgasm not as a physical chore, but as a gift, as a shared experience, as love.

Your partner pees on a lot of plastic sticks. They never give you the answer you want. You imagine the plastic sticks in a landfill somewhere, or dumped in the sea, that single line of disappointment gradually being bleached away by the sun, sinking into the deepest water, coming to rest on the freezing ocean floor or in the belly of a fish, polluting, useless, hateful.

Your donor can't come every month now. One fertile day passes away, and then another. But you can't complain. He's helping you and you're grateful for that. He has a life. He has a job and friends and a family and hobbies, some involving wood grain and some not. You know he contains multitudes, but you're not interested in any of them. You're interested in sperm.

Every fertile day that passes without him visiting, you think: Was that it? Was that the one? Was that your chance? But it slips away, and you work and your partner works and then you both have dinner and watch Netflix and go to sleep and wake up the next day and do it all over again and wait, wait, wait.

You daydream about your partner being pregnant. How she'll look, the beautifully inflated belly, the glowing skin. You dress her up in your mind, trying different maternity outfits, but the floral tents and fitted neutral vests look equally unfamiliar on her; as soon as you get a positive test, you'll do research into gender-neutral maternity clothes, something boxy and Scandinavian, something more her. You think about the plans you'll make, the new space you'll make in your lives and home. What you'll do for her: the foot rubs, the back rubs. The midnight trips to the supermarket to satisfy a craving. Holding her hand in the hospital as she has contractions. Holding the newborn baby in your arms.

Nothing happens. You and your partner try as often as you can, as often as her body and your donor's schedule will allow. Nothing and nothing and nothing. You struggle to convey in words the depth of your despair, the heat of your rage. You hate everyone who has a baby. You hate everyone who is pregnant. You want to say that that's not true, that you're glad they've got something that you understand the desire for, that you're happy for them. But you're not.

It's because you did something wrong. You're not sure what, but it must be something. When you were a teenager you saw a therapist, for your compulsive tics and your depression and your self-harming and your suicide attempt, and you said to the therapist, *It's because I'm bad.* The therapist asked you what you had done that was so bad, and you couldn't specify. Couldn't she see? It wasn't that you'd done or said anything bad. It's that you just were bad. You weren't sexually assaulted or beaten or belittled or left cold or hungry or alone or afraid. Nothing particularly awful had ever happened to you that might neatly explain why you wanted to die. You knew the therapist didn't believe this. She asked leading questions about your dad or uncle or teacher doing inappropriate things, but there was nothing. You almost wished there was something, so you'd have a reason. You just wanted to know why you felt so bad, when other people seem to feel fine. You just want to know why you and your partner can't have a baby, when other people get to have them.

You go on holiday together, just the two of you in a quiet house in the countryside. There's a pool, and every morning you float in the water, watching the clouds drift above you. Some mornings it rains and you love that even more; the feel of the rain on your face, your ears beneath the water, the sound of your own heartbeat. Sometimes your partner swims too and you float together, hands held like sleeping otters.

You take her out for lunch and some window-shopping. It's the first day she can get a pregnancy test result. She goes to the toilet in the café and comes out with the test tucked into the pocket of her denim dungaree dress. She can't bear to look, so you do. You see the single line, shake your head, put your arms around her. She nods, pretends there aren't tears in her eyes, and takes the test from you. Five minutes later you're in a shop, rattling clothes hangers, smelling scented candles, trying on rings, trying your best to think about nothing, and she leans in close to you and pulls the test out of her pocket: *Look!* The second line is faint. So faint that you didn't even see it. But she's right. It's there. A line. Faint, but there.

She's pregnant. Really, actually pregnant.

You go out for a fancy dinner to celebrate and she happily declines wine. She has a steak – for the iron, and also because she likes steak – with great mash. She says that several times: *Great mash*. Later, when you get back to the house, you float together in the pool, watching the tiny distant lights of stars and planes and satellites. You float, and you think of the hope inside her, no bigger than the dot of a star, floating too.

The dog knows immediately. She can smell it. She's extra-gentle with your partner; doesn't jump up, doesn't rush, doesn't headbutt her belly when looking for pats; just sits quietly at her feet, guarding, ready.

Your partner buys approximately a million pregnancy tests. She pees on them every morning and night, waiting for the second line to appear, stronger and clearer each day. She writes the dates and times on them in Sharpie and lays them out on the dining table. You sit there together for meals, in company with the tests, the cheery lines, the stacking up of days.

As the pregnancy progresses, you keep waiting to transcend. To feel more connected to life and death. But mostly it's just the same as before, except your partner has weird moods and snores loudly. You like that. Not the snoring specifically, but the ordinariness. Of course there's a baby coming. That's what you wanted, isn't it? That's what you hoped for, what you wished for. You put your desire out into the world, and the world provided, just like that.

You know it's not actually a baby, not yet; that it will only be a baby when it's outside your partner's body. You know it's a zygote, then a blastocyst, then an embryo, then a foetus. You know, because you googled it, that it's currently at the embryo stage. You know that it will only become a foetus around the time you go for your first scan. But this baby has been wanted and planned and hoped for and dreamt of for a long time. To you and your partner right now, this little bundle of cells: it's a baby.

You don't tell anyone about the pregnancy. You're in a bubble together. Everything sparkles. Everything gleams. The whole time feels blessed, peaceful. It's all falling into place. You really can have everything you want.

3

At the ten-week scan, you're annoyed because you have to wait for an hour. You wish you'd worn a different dress; this one is too short, and you feel uncomfortable. You're annoyed about an email you received earlier; you're eager to send a cold reply, and you compose it in your head as you wait. *When we get the scan picture,* your partner says, *I'll send it to my mum at the same time you send it to yours.* You agree; better than telling one before the other. You're excited to see the scan photo, but this doesn't feel like a big moment to you; just another routine step on the way to getting the baby. You discuss whether to announce it on social media; your partner doesn't mind, as she barely uses it anyway, but you're trying to move away from sharing personal information

online. *I think I want to*, you say. You want to tell everyone, to share the happy news: look, everyone. Look what
we made. Look how lucky we are.

In the room, you sit on a plastic chair while your partner
lies on the bed. The sonographer puts the scanner on her
belly. You see something on the screen. You can't tell what
it is. The sonographer doesn't say anything.

She goes out of the room to get someone else. They both
look at the screen. They still won't say anything. You and
your partner know something is wrong. You don't know
what the shapes on the screen are or what they mean. It's
a foreign language in unfamiliar script. All you know
is that something is wrong. You keep thinking please
please please even though you don't believe in any gods
so you don't know who you're talking to. But it doesn't
matter if there are gods or not, and it doesn't matter if you
say please.

I'm sorry, the sonographer says. *There's no heartbeat.*

You and your partner are put in a little beige room.
They're going to check again, but they have to get a different machine. You're gasping and crying so hard you
can't breathe. You keep thinking: It's not fair. It's not
fair. There's a little flat-pack table in the room, piles of

dog-eared leaflets. You want to push the leaflets to the floor, flip the table, slam the door. You need some drama, some noise. How can this be happening, and yet nothing is happening? But you sit obediently in your plastic chair, and cry.

Your partner is taken back to the scan room so that they can use the other machine. A nurse comes in to check on you. She says she recognises you. *Are you a translator?* she says. *Do you work here? I'm sure I know your face.* You say, still crying, that you must just have one of those faces. Later, after they do the other scan, after you know for sure it's hopeless, after you know the baby is dead, the nurse realises where she knows you from: a Halloween reading you did in an old burlesque hall for BBC radio a few years ago. Your face is swollen and red. Your head throbs from the force of your crying. But still you try to smile and talk with her about the Halloween event, because you want her to remember the version of you from then, and not from now. Wasn't the event fun? Weren't the old burlesque photos fun? Aren't ghost stories fun?

It's called a missed miscarriage. The baby has died but your partner's body is still holding on to it. She's sent home with some pills to take; you understand them to be the same pills you'd take for an abortion. Neither you nor your partner has ever had an abortion; you haven't needed to.

At home, you both go into the front room. You sit in the chair in the corner, the one your donor always sits in. Your partner says: *I want to go back*. You, thinking she means she wants to go back in time to when you both thought everything was okay, say: *I wish it was possible to go back too. No*, she says. *I want to go back to the hospital so they can check again in case the baby isn't really dead*. You feel it in your body when she says that. You didn't know that grief could be so physical; that it could literally throb in your chest.

You spend the weekend helping her. You try to provide everything she needs. You hold her in the shower while she cries. You make her tea with sugar to keep up her strength. You stroke her hair back from her forehead. You tell her it's okay, it's okay. All your emotion came out in that little beige room and now you are calm, unflappable, soothing.

The night before your partner finally miscarries, she dreams that a witch is trying to kill her baby fish by pulling it backwards in the water so it drowns.

Your mum and your partner's mum come round to help. They bring food, they make tea, they hold their crying daughters, and they cry too. To cheer you up, your mum tells you that a writer friend of yours – currently pregnant – has won a prize. You were also being considered for that prize. That's how you find out that you didn't win: by finding out that your friend did. You hate your friend. You hate her so intensely. You want something bad to happen to her baby. The thought that she will find out about the miscarriage and pity you fills you with rage. You want to go back now, soften that thought, say that you don't really want something bad to happen to her baby, that would be monstrous. But in that moment, that's exactly what you want.

Your mum puts her arm around you and you shrug her off, sob, stand up from the couch, walk around the room just to have something to do, wish you could shrug off your entire skin and be somewhere else, be someone else. You ask your mum, you scream at your mum, why would she tell you that, why would she tell you good news about someone else's life, why would she think you want to hear about anything but other people's misfortune?

You think you apologised to your mum later. Surely you did. But you can't remember doing it.

The miscarriage is the second worst thing that's happened in your life, the first being your dad's death seven years previously, just before you met your partner. You didn't see that coming either. When the phone rang that morning you thought it was your dad calling you back, as you'd just left a message on his answering machine. You answered, voice sing-songing. Heard your uncle's voice say *intensive care*. You'd just put bread in the toaster. Your sock had a hole in the toe. You got lost on the way to—

But you've already written that story. You've written about your dad dying, and about your grief over it, and you called it *The Old Asylum in the Woods at the Edge of the Town Where I Grew Up*. That got rid of it, didn't it? That helped, didn't it? You made it into a story. It's a book; it's got covers and page numbers. Strangers have read it. They know about your dad's death. And does that help? Does it help you to write it and does it help them to read it?

Now strangers can know about your baby's death too.

Your partner wants to see the baby when it comes out. All you want is to not see it. She calls you into the bathroom to see it. You look, and you think you will never forgive her for making you look.

It's impossible to describe grief. We keep trying – every writer, every grieving person tries. Perhaps that's the draw of it. We put it into words, into neat little paragraphs, we make the prose flow and the metaphors shine, and so our awkward, messy, ugly, unavoidable grief is made neat. Look: haven't you made it look nice? Haven't you written a little pitch document and sent it to an editor and got an advance and a contract and a deadline? Haven't you made it work for you? Your loss. Your agony. The gaping hole inside you. Here it is. It has a pretty cover. Please buy it.

4

Your partner goes back to work, and so do you. You get up early in the morning, make coffee, get stuck in. You're partway through a novel and there's a lot of research to do, about what people ate in the Middle Ages, about what people did about their periods, about the various diseases or mishaps that could cause a child to die, about what people said and wrote about their children dying, about how people lit their rooms after dark, about exactly how dark it could get in a forest on a winter's night, about what happens to a person when they're kept underground for an extended period of time in the dark. You learn that in the Middle Ages, a lot of babies died. It was dark a lot.

For several hours you sit and work at the kitchen table that you use as a desk. Then at 3 p.m. you take migraine medication you don't need and fall asleep listening to true crime podcasts. You need death to soothe you. The naps are short, but instant and deep, like a well.

You and your partner watch TV box sets every evening. You like them because they're never-ending and they stop you thinking. You and your partner are careful with one another. Polite, cautious, gently affectionate. You don't ask each other how you feel, because you already know, and there's nothing you can do about it anyway.

You and your partner go back to the hospital. She needs a scan to make sure the baby is out. You talk to the nurse about chicken and kale sausages from Whole Foods, which you're planning to have for your dinner tonight, and which you assure her are delicious, nutritious and reasonably priced. For her dinner the nurse is planning to have sushi with her husband. The baby is out.

You get back in touch with your donor to tell him about the miscarriage. You haven't messaged him for almost three months; the silence at first felt fizzing, giggling, like a child with a secret. You were hoping that the next time you messaged him it would be to send the scan photo. He agrees to help you again.

Even though you're terrified of flying and often have panic attacks during take-off, every night you and your partner fall asleep to a podcast about plane crashes. You've never heard the end of an episode. You've barely heard the start, it puts you to sleep so quickly.

Your partner wants to tell people about the miscarriage. She wants to speak about it publicly, to help herself and also maybe to help others, to form connection and solidarity. She says: *No one told me this could happen. Why did no one tell me?*

You realise that the advice to keep pregnancy a secret until after the first scan is because miscarriage in the first trimester is common, and that way you won't have to tell anyone when you miscarry. *Why the fuck shouldn't I tell anyone?* she says. *I won't let it be a secret; I won't let it be shameful.*

She writes an essay about her experience and you share it on your social media. You get a lot of replies; a huge number of people you know, both with and without children, have suffered miscarriage or infertility. You had no idea. Of course you had no idea. You understand that everyone has the right to keep their pain private, to speak or not speak about whatever they want, but still you think: I wish someone had told us.

But then: would you have listened? Or would you have thought: Them, not us. Never us.

A lot of people reassure you that it will be okay; that they lost a baby, or several babies, but it all worked out because look, they have children now, healthy growing ones, alive ones. You find this to be the most well-intentioned and least helpful thing to say. You don't care about their babies. You don't care about babies you and your partner might have in the future. You care about this baby: the one that died. That is the only baby you want.

Your partner is obsessed with the flats opposite. They caught on fire just after Christmas, four months ago. Everyone got out safely, but the flats were damaged. They're still empty. One of the windows has been left wide open, through rain and snow and windstorms. The blind is burnt and ripped, and it flaps out through the window. In the evenings, when you're watching another TV box set about something, you don't even know what, you catch your partner looking not at the TV but at that open window. The blind is very damaged now. It's almost gone.

One morning you ask your partner to bring you your glasses so you can read in bed; she comes in wearing them, with a Harry Potter lightning bolt drawn in eyeliner on her forehead and LUMOS MAXIMA scrawled across her bare breasts. Later she sings Sia songs in the shower and you lurk at the door, trying to absorb her voice, trying to absorb the moment, trying to cling to it even as it fades.

The second time your partner is pregnant, she tells you soon after you've woken, when you're having coffee and reading in bed. She hands you the test wordlessly. You hold it tight, hold her tighter.

She miscarries five days later in the supermarket. You've just put a rotisserie chicken and frozen peas in the trolley. *Do you want to leave?* you ask. *No*, she says, *let's just finish the shopping.* She cries silently while trying to find ox cheek in the fridge section.

You're grateful to your donor but you also resent him. Not him, but the need for him. You wish you could make your partner pregnant. You wish that you could make a child together and not need anyone else. You wish you didn't have to rely on others, on random kind strangers, to achieve this most basic of human desires.

But is he kind? Is he altruistic and generous, doing this only to help others despite the inconvenience to himself? Or is he nefarious and egotistical, doing this for some perverted reason only he knows? You tangle yourself up in knots, thinking about why we donate anything to anyone else, what we lose from it and what we gain from it. But ultimately, when it comes to your donor, it doesn't matter. You want a baby. You need sperm; he's got it; he's willing to let you have it. It doesn't matter why he's helping you. It just matters that he is.

More fertile days pass unmarked. More months with no attempt at a baby. But this time it's not your donor; it's your partner. She's losing hope. She doesn't want to try; she can't take the feeling of it not working. You stop messaging the donor to ask him about dates. He ghosts you, you ghost him; you become ghosts to one another. You wonder if he ever wonders about those tiny scraps of life he helped your partner make. Miscarriage is common and he must have begun as many unsuccessful as successful pregnancies. You picture him, taking notes in his physiotherapy lectures, photographing his wood grains, drinking a pint with his friends, brushing his teeth and regarding his reflection in the bathroom mirror. Does he think then of the babies, born and unborn?

Well, do you ever think of the people walking around with your blood in their bodies? No, you don't. Not properly. When you're sitting there in the blood donor centre watching the little plastic bag fill and expand. Crumpling up the foil of a teacake afterwards while they make sure you won't faint. Later that evening, when you peel the sticking plaster off your inner elbow. When the letter comes in reminding you it's time to donate again: then you might think of them, in an abstract sort of way. You have friends who had difficult labours and needed blood, and you've thought that it would be nice if they'd got yours. It would also be nice if someone who isn't your friend got yours. It would even be nice if someone completely awful got yours. You don't actually care; you've never really thought about it. You go, you donate, you walk away feeling mildly altruistic. Perhaps that's what he does too.

You decide that the problem is the donor. His sperm is weak. There's not enough of it. It's the wrong type. It's the wrong shape. It's the wrong size. It's not compatible with your partner's body. You have to blame him; it's too hard to blame no one.

New sperm will work, your partner says, and you agree. You just have to get some.

For years you haven't really noticed men, but now they're catching your eye all the time. You're obsessed. Whenever you see an attractive man, you think: Sperm donor. You see a man on the train. Scruffy beard, thick honey-coloured biceps. You want to say: *Can you help me and my partner? You've heard about donating blood – well, this is similar, except—*

No.

Do you want to come to ours and—

No.

If you've got sperm, and you're not using it, could—

No.

Impossible to not make this sound like bad porn or a scam.

You go to Malaysia for a book festival and meet Adam, a ridiculously beautiful Chinese man with the same birthday as you. He has a freckle on his lower lip. He wants to live in India. He was in finance but now works for a women's empowerment charity. You think about asking him to be your donor. You genuinely consider the cost of a flight from Kuala Lumpur to Glasgow every month, plus a hotel, plus any other expenses he might have. Can you afford it? Would he agree to it? How would you broach this with your partner without making it sound exactly as insane as it is? Thankfully you regain your senses and simply pass a pleasant evening chatting with Adam, and never once mention sperm.

You start dreaming about men. Long, elaborate, vivid dreams, often sexual. You're never yourself in the dreams.

You dream you're a teenager with a brooding, lanky, drug-addicted boyfriend you try to save. You dream you're a gay man torn between the love of two brothers. You dream you're at a wedding full of strangers where you know you've had an affair with the bride or groom but you don't know which. You dream you're an American woman kidnapped and held in a man's basement. You dream you're a woman who regularly sleeps with her uncle. Usually you tell your partner everything, but you don't tell her about the dreams.

You go to Manchester for a Pride event. You read one of your first stories, about a girl who dumped you when you were twenty-three, and the period sex scene from your last novel. After the interval you have to do a video interview and then it's too late for you to go in and see the performers; instead you hang out in the empty bar and have a large glass of wine because they've run out of small glasses.

You scroll blankly through your phone, opening apps and closing them again. Emails: nothing. Social media: ugh. Games: no. You know your own tendency towards digital self-harm, and you feel a building temptation to look yourself up on Goodreads and read the 1-star reviews. You could just put your phone down. But who ever just puts their phone down? Then you'd have to live in the real world, and it's terrible there. Desperate for distraction, entertainment, anything, you open the calendar app and notice the date. A year ago today you thought your partner was pregnant, but the baby was already dead.

After the Pride event you meet a friend of a friend with her baby, who is gorgeous and grinning. As you hold the baby you think, momentarily, about stealing it. It's a cute baby. It has a cute face and cute hands. Most importantly, it's alive. The imp of the perverse, you tell yourself. And anyway, you don't want that baby. You want the baby you're still convinced you can have with your partner.

You identify a potential new donor, a friend's partner. He's healthy, handsome, intelligent, sensitive. He loves children but doesn't want his own. You can't imagine a more perfect donor.

You all meet up in a cocktail bar. You've already run this by your friend as a hypothetical and received a yes, and the friend ran it by the partner and got a yes from him too. You all know why you're here. You all know what question is coming, and what the answer will be. You chitchat about work, about books you're reading, about whatever horrible thing is in the news. Your heart beats hard. He's going to say yes. He's already had time to think about it and discuss it with his partner and read the legal leaflet you passed on. He's definitely going to say yes. But what if he says no. *Seen any good TV box sets lately?* you ask. The cocktails are botanical, stupid-expensive, dizzy-strong. You finish two before your friend says: *For fuck's sake, you are ridiculous, just get it over with.*

He says yes.

You start trying right away, with your now well-practised at-home method.

Nothing happens. You try again; nothing. You try again; still nothing. Then you have to stop trying; the country has gone into lockdown due to the Covid-19 pandemic. But it's okay, or it's all very much not okay, but in terms of the baby it's okay, because you're finally at the top of the IVF waiting list. IVF always works. Everyone knows it's the last-ditch guarantee, the thing that works when nothing else will. It won't be long now until you have a baby.

After your partner's first IVF injection, you expect mood swings and night sweats. But, nothing. She's fine. Euphoric even; blissful. She says: *I don't understand why people say these IVF meds are bad; I feel fine.*

But then she has the progesterone pessary. Now she's too hot in the night, restless, cramping, moody. She's exhausted but can't sleep. She's hungry but nauseated. You make her scrambled eggs, no cheese, no mustard, no toast. She wants plainer eggs. *I just need space*, she says, and then when you go to leave the room she says: *Wait, where are you going?* You try to do all the things she asks, even the ones that contradict each other. She says: *I don't understand why no one tells you about the pessary.*

Because of lockdown, your partner has to go to the hospital alone for all her IVF treatments. It's strange, she says, because it's all so clinical. You have to put on a hospital gown, she says, and then walk alone down a long empty white corridor, and outside every door is a big pile of brightly coloured Crocs; everything has to be sterile so the staff all change their shoes before going in. The room is like a regular operating theatre but there's a steel hatch, a little serving window, where the bits of your body are passed to and from the lab. You lie down on the bed, she says, and they count you out and you're all having a laugh about brownies; and that's just typical for your partner, you think; she would be chatting to them and charming them, she doesn't see them as just nurses, functional figures, she never sees people like that, she always sees people in the fullness of themselves. Then you wake up, she says, and it's all done, and you're in a different room full of curtained beds, and you get toast and tea, and they come and tell you how the egg retrieval went, and while you wait you can hear people getting their news on the other side of the curtain. She hears the woman at the end, who sounds young and happy, be told that she only got three eggs and they're not good ones. She hears another woman be told that she got four eggs. Then it's her turn: eight eggs, they say, and all good eggs, excellent eggs. You feel like you've won a prize then, she says. The woman at the end, the woman with the three bad eggs, is sobbing aloud like someone has died, but really it's that someone hasn't lived.

Your anxiety, which usually exists as groundwater burbling around ankle level, floods up to your chest. You can feel it pressing on your lungs. Your compulsive tics, which haven't bothered you for a decade, return. You wake up at 5 a.m. every day, terrified of dying. Your gums ache. Your eyes itch. Your hand shakes.

The IVF people call: you got a good embryo. Eight good eggs, one good embryo. Well, you only need one. And it's a really good one. Your partner goes alone again, down the long empty white corridor, a different one this time, though it also has a pile of Crocs. She sits alone in a series of rooms, moving from one to the other when she's told to, giving her name and date of birth over and over. The rooms must be in a square around the lab somehow because they all have a little silver window that looks into the lab; she laughs that she feels like she's at a drive-through, and even the consultant laughs; that's so like her, you think, of course she'd charm them all, and surely that will help, surely they'll like her so much they'll work extra hard for the embryo. She's awake for this part, and she comes home excited: *I watched it!* she says. *I could see it on the screen; I watched them put the embryo directly into my fallopian tube, it went right in there. How couldn't it work?* She says: *Science is cool.*

Parts of this journey are for you both. But there are parts that are just for her. You weren't in that long white corridor. You weren't in that room. You're not in her body. That part is hers alone.

You've written a series for BBC radio about the history of ghosts, and you go into the Glasgow studio to record it. Due to lockdown, the studios are empty. You have to get your temperature checked every time you go into the building; even if you pop out to the coffee van, you still have to get rechecked on your way back in. There are arrows on the floor; to go to the loo you have to circle around the entire building, seeing no one, hearing no one. You thought that the producer would be in a neighbouring studio, that you'd be able to see her through the internal window. But she's on the other side of the building, and you communicate only through headphones. The neighbouring studio is empty, lights off, the window reflecting black.

The IVF fails. You want to write more about that, to create a picture, to explain how you both felt. But you can't. It hurts. Even now, it still hurts.

You tell your donor that it didn't work. He's done so much to help you. This time it was a lot more than ejaculating into a cup in your bathroom. It was multiple hospital visits. Blood tests. Semen tests. Counselling sessions with his partner. Counselling sessions with you and your partner. He did all of that, and all he ever thought he was going to get out of it was the joy and satisfaction of helping someone get what they most wanted in the world.

But as it happened, he didn't even get that. And neither did you.

You go back to the IVF clinic to speak to the doctor. You're allowed to go with your partner this time. In the waiting room there are three other couples. You've sat in this waiting room before. You remember looking around at the other people and finding it interesting that they were all struggling to conceive. You realised that even if you had sperm, even if it was possible for you and your partner to make a baby together, there's still a chance you couldn't. Sometimes it just doesn't happen, and no one will ever be able to tell you why.

You google 'IVF success rates' on your phone: 20–35 per cent. And the likelihood of a pregnancy decreases with each successive round. Only one couple in this waiting room will actually end up with a baby.

No one ever told you that. No one ever told you that it was more likely you wouldn't get a baby. Or they did tell you, and you didn't listen.

The doctor says you're entitled to two more IVF cycles. In the past three years, your partner has had three miscarriages and a failed IVF cycle. She wants a baby more than anything in the world. *I can't do it again*, she says.

If she hadn't had the miscarriages. If she hadn't made it as far as the scan. If it hadn't come out looking like something. She just can't do it again. *I won't cope*, she says. What's more important to you: a baby or your partner, intact? You choose her. You agree to no more IVF.

The doctor says that if all you want is a healthy baby, your best chance is to go with the younger womb, the younger eggs. Meaning, yours. Meaning, you.

5

You start trying with your body as soon as you can. You track your periods and pee on plastic ovulation sticks.

Your partner asks if you want her to help you orgasm. She knows how, after all. *No*, you say. *I just want to get it done.*

Your donor masturbates in your bathroom and leaves the cup of semen politely on the toilet tank. Your partner carries it through to your bedroom tucked in her bra to keep it at body temperature. Now it's your turn to masturbate functionally. Your partner takes a photo of you afterwards, your body in plough position on the bed, your hips in your hands, your legs curving round towards your head, your cunt to the ceiling. Go in, you try to mentally transmit to the sperm. Go IN.

For the next two weeks, until it's possible to take a pregnancy test, you're Schrödinger's pregnant woman: there
both is and is not an embryo inside you. All you can do is
wait. No one, including you, can know what's happening
inside your body.

You have to act as if you're pregnant, because you might
be. No coffee. No alcohol. No unpasteurised cheese. No
cured meat. No soft-boiled eggs. Somehow, when it was
your partner avoiding all these things, it seemed easy. You
linger in the dairy aisle at the supermarket, staring at the
Brie. You fantasise about charcuterie boards, the tissue-
thin cured meats, curled like roses in shades of madder,
crimson, carmine. You imagine a soft yolk breaking sunny
on your tongue.

There are plenty of other things you shouldn't do. Hot tubs.
Smoking. Eating steak tartare. Cleaning out cats' litter
boxes. But those aren't things you'd be doing anyway, even
if you weren't trying to get pregnant. The only thing you
really miss is caffeine. You've gone from two double espressos
per day to two cups of decaf tea a day. And you're fucking
pissed about it. You make your partner a strong coffee every
morning so you can stick your nose into the bag of beans.

You become obsessed with your vagina. Are your labia
swollen because you've been sitting on a hard chair for too

long, or because you're pregnant? Is there a bit of blood on the toilet paper because vaginas just bleed sometimes, or is it implantation and you're pregnant? Does your discharge smell different because you've put semen in it for the first time in a decade, or because you're pregnant?

As the week progresses, your obsession expands to your whole body. Are you tired because it's 2020 and everything is terrible, or because you're pregnant? Do you feel a bit sick because you just realised there's some dog shit mashed into your shoe, or because you're pregnant?

It's four days until Christmas. You imagine showing your mum the positive test and saying, *Happy Christmas!*, her joyful tears, how she'll want to hug you but can't, how you and your partner will have made something positive from the general horror of 2020.

You feel pregnant.

You think you might be pregnant.

So easy! First time! Well done you!

Your story is working out so neatly, so perfectly. It was meant to be.

The baby will be born in August. You don't love the thought of being heavily pregnant through the summer, but that's okay. You can put up a paddling pool in your mum's garden and spend all day with your feet soaking in cold water. You can eat ice lollies and wear a big sunhat, big enough to cast a shadow over your bump. You probably won't need summer clothes as you won't be leaving the house much in the early weeks, but you can get some really cute autumn and winter clothes. A little baby coat. A little baby hat with ear flaps. A little baby Halloween outfit, a little baby Christmas outfit. You wonder if the baby will grow up to prefer Halloween or Christmas. If the baby will prefer drawing or numbers. How long it will take for the baby to smile, to crawl, to say *mummy*. You cradle your belly, dreaming.

Your belly cramps. You know immediately. You've felt those cramps every month since you were twelve. Your period.

Your partner gets a scratch card as part of her secret Santa gift from work. You scratch off the silver panels and you win £40,000. Then you realise you've misread the instructions, and you haven't actually won anything.

Christmas happens. Hogmanay happens. You drink too much and tell yourself, Hey, this is great, how nice to be able to drink too much. You think your New Year's resolutions could involve steak tartare, cat shit and smoking. Well, why not? Why the fuck not?

You try again the next month. You feel a simmering rage beneath your skin all the time. You feel like a greyhound being held back before a race begins. Chafing. Frustrated. Impatient. And angry, so angry. When your partner wasn't pregnant you didn't feel angry, just sad. But now you feel like you could burst into flames at any moment. Why can't you get pregnant? Why can't you and your partner have this? Why is it so easy for everyone else? Why does it have to be the same fucking thing, over and over and over? Why can't something just happen?

It doesn't happen that month either. You are surprised to look in the mirror and see you're not actually on fire.

You have very little memory of the things you said and did in those not-pregnant weeks, which is probably for the best.

You realise getting pregnant isn't something you can choose to do, like you can choose to move your hand or shut your eyes. It happens in your body, but you can't make your body do it.

You don't want to start anything. You can't plan anything. You're just waiting. To distract yourself, you watch horror films. Mostly pregnancy horror. You'd never thought of it as being a particularly populous genre, but it turns out that when you go looking for it, there's enough to fill an entire two-week wait. You want to give yourself something to fear, because you're feeling it anyway. It's easier to direct it outwards than inwards.

You've been trying to shake off a sinus infection for two weeks, but it just won't go away. Your face aches all the time, your cheekbones, your jaw, your eye sockets. One evening you finally manage to relax, and realise your sinuses aren't actually infected any more. You've just been clenching your jaw and forehead so hard that it's made all your bones ache.

You know you're not pregnant. You don't feel pregnant. You're annoyed that you can't have coffee or wine when you already know it won't matter. But you could be. You could be. That hope, so tempting, already turning bitter.

On the first morning after the two-week wait, you go into the bathroom and pee on the plastic stick. There's a second line, very faint. You wipe and wash your hands. Your heart is beating very hard. You take the test through to the bedroom and hold it out to your partner. You say: *Can you see that line?* She looks at it. She cries out. *Yes*, she says. *Yes!*

You can't stop crying and you don't know if it's happy tears or terrified tears. Your partner can't stop holding the positive test. She props it up beside the bed so she can look at it as she falls asleep and when she wakes up.

You are pregnant. You are pregnant!

The Growing

1

The symptoms start almost immediately. You look exactly the same, but you don't feel the same.

- You feel like horrible bread dough.

- You feel like a half-boiled potato.

- You feel like you have been inflated.

- You feel like someone is poking your insides with pins.

- You feel like you need to fart and shit a lot.

- You feel shooting pains in your vagina, in the fronts of your thighs, in your ovaries (you assume; you don't know exactly where your ovaries are).

- You feel like you've just run a marathon, not that you've ever run a marathon, not that you've ever run further than you were forced to in PE at school, but that's the only way you can describe the exhaustion, the bone-deep brain-deep exhaustion you feel in your entire body.

- You feel like you're feeling all these things for no reason because you're going to miscarry anyway so it's all for nothing.

You lie on the couch all day watching horror films and exchanging chatty voice notes with friends. You haven't told them about your positive test. It's not that you wouldn't tell them if you miscarried. You just want to keep it close for now. You don't want it to be happening in the world, but only in your body. In your body, maybe you can keep it safe. The pains come and go, but the pains feel good. The pains mean there's still a pregnancy. They feel like something is happening. Finally, something is happening.

Every time you leave the house, you imagine being stabbed by a random person, being hit by a car, being mugged, being punched in the belly after getting caught in a sudden fight (although none of these things have ever happened to you). You imagine yourself gasping out: *Please – I'm pregnant*. Or you imagine someone politely telling you there's something on the seat of your jeans – then bleeding out in the middle of the street. You imagine the baby with teeth and claws, biting its way out. As a fiction writer, you make your living with your imagination. It's the most precious thing you have, the thing you most value in yourself. But sometimes you hate it. You hate how easy it is for your brain to imagine everything that could go wrong, then play it out for you in sensory detail, surround sound, scents and tastes, textures and temperatures, more real than life. Sometimes you'd like to know what it's like to only live in reality. To only think about what's actually there.

You wouldn't say *I'm pregnant* even if you did get stabbed. You can't even say *I'm pregnant* to your partner. You can't even say it to yourself. Acknowledging it might make it go away. You know that's magical thinking, but what is a six-week embryo if not magical thinking? It's the size of a grain of rice. It's the size of a single lentil, a pomegranate seed, the little black eraser on the top of a mechanical pencil, a ladybird, the head of a pushpin, a daisy petal, an earring back, a teardrop. It's absolutely nothing. And it's everything.

You tell your mum about the pregnancy on a freezing winter day in the park. Lockdown is still in full force and you're not allowed to be inside with her, so you both bundle up, get takeaway hot chocolate, and climb the steepest hill. At the top, you sit together on a bench. Your heart is beating hard. Your mum is talking about how she's going to clear out her knitwear, how she's got a new 1,000-piece jigsaw, how she's really got into making casseroles, how she's desperately doing anything she can to distract herself from how shit and scary the world is right now. *I've got something that might help*, you say. You take the positive pregnancy test out of your pocket and show it to her. At first she thinks it's a Covid test and says, *Oh no*. Then she realises what it is and says, in a different tone, *No! No!* She immediately starts crying and reaches out for you. *I don't care about distance*, she says.

A list of your food cravings, during which period your partner nicknames you the Very Hungry Caterpillar, and all of which last for a brief moment during which they are the only thing you can possibly imagine eating, after which they are repulsive and can't be thought of or named aloud:

- Three (it must be exactly three) hash browns with cheese and sriracha

- Peach slices and berries, warmed in a pan, drizzled with a little cream and honey

- Toasted croissant with 'sharp jam'

- Potato waffles with cottage cheese

- An apple (halfway through eating the apple you suddenly can't bear it, you can't even have it in the room with you, you make your partner throw it in the garden)

- Two boiled eggs, chopped up with butter, mixed with cold cooked white rice and chicken

- 'Meat paste' (you want meat, but meat is too solid, and although you've never had meat paste in your life it seems like the only logical thing to eat)

- An apple, again

- Potatoes

- Potatoes

- Potatoes

- Potatoes

You cry because you're worried you're eating too much potato. You cry because you're tired all the time, and you're sick of sleeping, and sleeping doesn't stop you feeling tired. You cry because you're not writing anything and you don't even want to write anything, and if you're not writing then you don't know who you are. You cry because you watched a documentary about the Yorkshire Ripper and you're thinking about how he killed all those women and it's just so unfair that they were out there living their lives and it was all ruined because of some sad man. You cry because you're crying about everything. You cry because the only reason you're crying about everything is that you're pregnant and you don't look pregnant and you can't tell people that you're pregnant because you're going to miscarry anyway so if you tell them you'll have to tell them about the miscarriage too and you don't think you can bear to do that again.

You keep seeing something at the bottom edge of your peripheral vision. First you thought you saw a large black beetle crawling on your arm. Then the tip of a black cat's tail as it walked behind the coffee table. Then, when you were reading in bed at night, a very small bat creeping around your bedside lamp. Of course, every time you look, there's nothing there.

A lazy afternoon. You have some email responses to send, a TV show to watch so you can review it on the radio, some minor edits on a short story to check over. You make tea, humming to yourself. You still feel sick, but you've discovered that plain tortilla chips, eaten pretty much constantly, help. You're in week seven of the pregnancy, which is almost week eight, which is two months, which is nearly a quarter of the whole pregnancy, which feels like a huge step forward into safety. Every day that passes, your risk of miscarriage decreases. There's a website that gives you the miscarriage odds for each day of your pregnancy, and you check it at least once a day. You're struck by a sudden thought. You look at the calendar. Your anxiety floods up to your chest, choking you. You've miscalculated; you're only just starting week six. Any feeling of security and confidence disappears. It's so early. You're barely pregnant. You spent years fucking men and not tracking your period; you have no idea if it's ever been late. You could have been this pregnant before, many times even, and not even known; you could have had a very early miscarriage and thought it was just your period coming as normal. Is there even a heartbeat yet? When the heart starts beating, even though it's basically a tadpole without a brain, the chance of miscarriage drops. But are you even there? Is this even real? You're exhausted and aching and craving and crying, but you don't even know if it's real. The embryo is too small to see on a scan, so even if you could get a scan, it guarantees nothing, and no one can tell you if you'll miscarry, and no one knows what's happening inside your body, least of all you.

You feel sick and achy and exhausted. You're glad: still pregnant. You only want to eat crunchy things: apples, raw carrots, crunchy nut cornflakes, sour cream and chive crisps. They have to be ridged crisps. With a cup of tomato soup. Few food items make you feel sick now; you're back on boiled eggs, hot milk, steamed fish: things you couldn't even hear your partner mention last week. You now get nauseous from random objects, specifically a nice jigsaw your partner got you, and an audiobook you were listening to. You can't even bear to look at the jigsaw box or the audiobook app. Just the thought of them makes you feel sick.

Your partner takes you for a drive to distract you from feeling sick. Every thought feels like it's being dredged up through thick mud. In the car she's doing her best with you, talking to you, singing along to the radio, asking you about how you're feeling. You stare into space, saying nothing, thinking nothing. Your brain is a potato. You start crying. *I'm a potato*, you sob. *My potato*, she says, and takes your hand.

You start getting pins and needles in your breasts, which are swollen, very round and white and shiny, like a woman in an old painting. Your skin breaks out into spots, which upsets you as you had acne for many years and finally went on medication to get rid of it, which made your face bright red and your lips peel off in sheets, though it did get rid of the acne. You have an allergic reaction to something, and your eyes puff up like marshmallows so that you can't open them, and your cheeks and jaw are covered in tiny white pustules, and you can't take anything for it because you're pregnant, and you feel monstrous and uncomfortable and you're going to miscarry anyway so it's all for nothing.

You go to the toilet. You pee, you wipe. You brace yourself before looking at the toilet paper. You can sense your partner listening from the next room, pretending to be playing with her phone but really waiting for you to call *great TP!*, which you do. Great TP means no blood, no gore, no miscarried remnants of child.

With your partner, you don't have to translate. Partly it's just because of who she is, and who you are, and who you both are together. Partly it's because she's a woman. You could fall in love with anyone of any gender, you know that. You've had boyfriends, and they were fine. Some were a bit more than fine, and some were a bit less than fine, but you loved them. You pictured yourself marrying at least one of them. You think in a parallel universe, you did marry one of them. That now you have three sons and live out on the islands and teach English at a high school. That now you work as a bookseller and live in New Zealand and have a whole bunch of guinea pigs. That now you live somewhere

English and flat and green, and the Scottish burr has faded
from your accent, and you've grown your hair long, and
you always have painted nails, and you know how to make
roast dinners. You'd rankle slightly at your apparently
heteronormative life, though you suspect you'd be happy
enough. But you also suspect there would be something
missing. Or – something unsaid. Something you didn't
even know that you didn't know how to say. Something
that, with your partner, you say without even thinking, and
know it will be heard and understood. With a woman, for
you, it's just easier. There's no language barrier.

Being pregnant and in a relationship with someone who
has been pregnant is also easier. Most of the time you can't
even say it, you don't even know what it is you want to say,
but you don't need to. *I get it*, she says, making you tea,
stroking your swollen feet, bringing more plain tortilla chips
for you to slowly, grumpily chew. She gets the sickness, the
exhaustion, the randomly tingling body parts. She gets the
weird pains, the aches, and how you like them despite the
discomfort because they mean you're still pregnant. She gets
the impatience for it all to be over, for the baby to be here
already. She gets the fear that it's all going to be over.

How can you and your partner mourn the loss of her
babies, the loss of her whole fertility journey, while also
being grateful and excited for this new life, so easily made?

This isn't how either of you had planned for things to go. This isn't the baby you thought you'd have. This isn't the body you thought you'd make it with. But the world doesn't care about your plans, and neither does your body.

You haven't written anything for months, not since the IVF failed. You haven't written through the disappointment and injustice of the IVF, through the rage and impatience of trying to conceive, through the nausea and boredom of early pregnancy. But you're writing this. It might not be exactly what you had planned, but it's something.

You tell yourself: the thing inside you. It's not exactly what you planned. But it might be something.

2

Every time you drive through an intersection, you picture a speeding car running a red light and smashing into you. Every time you drive over a railway crossing, you picture the train smashing into you. You picture a piece of an aeroplane falling onto the car roof and crushing you. You picture a log slipping off the back of a lorry and smashing through the windscreen into you. You picture someone throwing a brick off a bridge and it shattering the window, the broken glass slicing your face and body, glittering in your hair. You picture the lights of the ambulance strobing blue across your skin. How carefully they'll lift you from the wreckage. How you'll tell the story of it after. If there is an after.

When you have these thoughts, you always make note of the song playing on the radio. Is this the song you want to be playing during your moments of tragedy or agony? You remember the feel of the too-short dress when you found out the baby was dead. The smell of the burning toast when you found out your dad was in intensive care. You know the stickiness of the last thing before a tragedy. Every now and then, if there's a certain taste in your mouth or a certain sound in your ears, you think: Will this stick?

You have a bleed. Small, dark. You and your partner had sex the previous night. Can you have come too hard? You google it and all the websites say that when you're pregnant your cervix is tender, and during sex it can become irritated and bleed. But nothing went near your cervix. There was no penis and no penetration. You phone the midwife and she explains to you, a little awkwardly, you think, which seems weird to you as she must talk about cervixes every day, about your cervix and how it's tender and can bleed. You explain about the no-penis situation. You ask if it's the penis that's the issue, or the orgasm. You wonder whether to try to explain about coming so hard that you genuinely think you could have dislodged an embryo from your uterus, but then you think maybe she's never had sex with a lesbian and won't get it. She books you in for an early scan.

You feel anxious. You feel upset. But you also feel vindicated. You knew this would happen. You're not allowed to have a baby. You're not allowed to have anything decent or good. You're so repulsed by yourself that you can't bear to look in the mirror. You hate your own mouth and everything inside it, everything that comes out of it. You want to crawl into a cave so no one has to see you. You can't believe that this body you hate, that you have spent years hating, could do something good. Why should this disgusting body be allowed to make a baby? Why should you be allowed to create something that's half you, when you are so repulsive?

It's five days until the scan. Your morning sickness is bad again. You tell yourself that's good. Morning sickness means hormones means still pregnant. You feel too sick to read or watch TV. You feel too sick to sleep or rest quietly. *Read me facts*, you say to your partner. She asks what you want facts about. *Anything*, you say. *Not babies*. She tries the random button in Wikipedia. She reads to you for hours while you lie with your face pressed into her side, breathing in the smell of her skin, feeling your nausea settle. You learn about the history of Prussia, about the kraken, about astraphobia, about Prehistoric geometry theories, about existentialism, about a rugby player in the 1930s called Beef Dancer, about the capture of Fort Erie. You retain exactly none of the information.

Later your partner drives to the bookshop and gets some books of facts. She stacks them up by her side of the bed. There are enough facts there to get you through a whole pregnancy. Three pregnancies, even. You're not sure if you'll even get to have one.

You haven't bled again. You still call *great TP!* through to your partner every time you go to the toilet.

You're reassured that the dog is still acting like you're pregnant. No jumping, no rushing, no bumping her head into you looking for pats. She just lies by your feet, tender, guarding. You realise there must be a point where she stopped acting in this extra-gentle way with your partner; a moment where the dog could smell that she was no longer pregnant. Whenever it was, neither of you noticed.

It's two days until the scan. You're desperate to stop thinking about your own body for a moment. Your partner takes you for a drive for a change of scene. All you feel capable of doing is going for very slow walks; she says at least you can go for a walk in a slightly different place. There's snow, a loch, and a mass of huge white wind turbines, slowly swooping round like something from an old sci-fi film. The dog frolics gleefully, chasing her ball into snowdrifts. Your partner takes great lungfuls of the winter air, holding your hand to help you over uneven parts of the path, telling an increasingly complex story about a sticky-label-based feud going on at her work. You eat plain tortilla chips. You walk very slowly. You feel sick.

You used to use a lot of talismans. For your first novel, which had a protagonist called North, you bought a small brass antique compass. Every day before you could start writing, you'd set the compass on your desk and turn it until the arrow pointed north. Your last novel was about a journey from a blue thermal pool across forests until, finally, ending at a black sand beach; for that one you bought a handmade ceramic spoon, the handle-tip of which was black and unglazed, rough as sand, and the bowl of which was a shiny, smooth glazed blue, like a pool of water. Every day you'd place it on your desk and rub your thumb from the rough end to the smooth end three times. Then you could start.

You don't have talismans now. Not for the book you're writing. Not for the embryo you're growing. You tell yourself that you don't need them any more, that you've moved past magical thinking. Every day when your partner goes to work, you pick up the pregnancy test from where it still sits by her side of the bed. You stare at it, making sure the second line is really there.

The scan is tomorrow. You've done nothing all week. You've failed to be productive but you've also failed to rest. You hate being pregnant. Hate it hate it hate it. When you were trying to get pregnant, you said to your friends: *Trying to get pregnant is the least fun thing I've ever done.* Now you know that being pregnant is the least fun thing. But you don't say it. You don't believe in God, ghosts, an afterlife, aliens, tarot, reiki, or anything supernatural or alternative whatsoever. But you also, somehow, believe that if you think or say certain things then it will affect real-world elements outside your control. If you say or think that you don't like being pregnant, someone or something will take it away from you.

In the waiting room for the scan there are four chairs, too close together. Three other women wait. One doesn't have a mask on and you try to subtly turn away from her and breathe shallowly. She keeps trying to talk to you all, awkwardly starting conversations about the weather, about the hospital, about the waiting room, about your pregnancies. You don't want to talk. You're anxious, trying to read a book on your e-reader to distract yourself; the PDF is corrupted and there are random numbers inserted on every page, but you like this as you have to focus hard to read, and it busies your brain. You're desperate for the toilet – they said to come in with a full bladder as it helps them to find the uterus, and if they say full bladder you're going to make yours as full as it can go. You're an overachiever even with your piss.

But you realise the chatty woman is also anxious; she deals with it in the opposite way. You put down your e-reader and talk to her, even if just to stop thinking about how much you need the toilet. You don't tell the woman anything about yourself or your pregnancy, not because you feel secretive, but because you don't know what to say. She says she's already had a scan, and now she's waiting for another. She's had positive pregnancy tests and she has plenty of symptoms. They can find the sac where the baby should be, but it's empty. Her hormone levels say she's pregnant, but there's no foetus there. For two months she's thought she's pregnant, but now she doesn't know if she ever was.

You get called into the scan room. You phone your partner; she wasn't allowed to wait in the waiting room with you, and she's been standing outside in a Glasgow winter for half an hour. She comes in shivering. You hold her cold hand. The sonographer finds your uterus quickly, says, *There it is!*, but not if there's a heartbeat. You and your partner are both thinking about last time. You squeeze her hand harder and she squeezes back. You can't believe it's happening again. How could it be happening again? It's not fair. It's not fair.

There's the heartbeat! the sonographer says, and you can see it, and it's strong. The little blurry tadpole blob has a fast pulsing heart. It's waving its hand nubs around. You cry, strong and sudden, the tears falling into your ears, onto the paper sheet.

You get a scan picture to take home. It's black-and-white, blurry, smaller than a postcard. It looks like a lunar landscape, like an old stone wall, like a scratched silver etching. The paper is shiny and picks up your fingerprints. You grip it tight.

On the way out you say *good luck* to the maskless woman in the waiting room; she sees you're holding a picture, and doesn't reply.

3

You have a series of dreams about normal-sized houses with very tiny doors. In one dream, it's an attic flat, enormous, cavernous, a ceiling so high that every sound echoes – but the entrance is a tiny tunnel you have to crawl through. It's so narrow that your shoulders and hips scrape the walls. You wonder how any of the furniture got inside. In another, it's your childhood home, a two-storey Georgian semi, but the front door is the little plasticky flap of the Wendy house you had when you were five. Birth dreams? Or lockdown dreams?

You're thinking about your dad. This morning your therapist, very gently, mentioned that when the baby is born, some of your unresolved feelings about your dad's death might surface. Things that you didn't deal with at the time, and thought you could go the whole rest of your life not dealing with. Because the baby might look a lot like your dad, because you look a lot like him. Because the baby doesn't have a dad. Because the baby represents the furthest reach of yourself; you have no grandparents, only one living parent; most of your genetic relatives live in other countries and despite the pull you feel towards them, you feel them drifting away; because the baby will pull them back, the call of blood to blood. Because you'll be a parent, and that will make you think about what that means, and what your own parents got right and wrong in their own parenting, and how they were parented as children, and so on all the way back. She's big into inherited trauma, your therapist. You didn't realise until that moment that your dad died ten years ago. Depending on how close to the due date the baby is born, it might be on the exact anniversary. You didn't realise. You wish you still hadn't realised. Now all you can think about is your dad. You're never not thinking about him, in a sense, because grief—

But you stop that thought before you can even finish a sentence, because it's not true. There are lots of times you're not thinking about your dad; of course there are. It would be bizarre to say otherwise. You weren't thinking about him yesterday when you felt so sick you couldn't raise your head from the pillow and bleated pathetically for your partner to please bring you some plain tortilla chips, which you then eat horizontally without raising your head from the pillow. You weren't thinking about him two months ago when you were trying to orgasm so your partner could squirt your friend's semen in your cunt in an attempt to get into the exact state you're in now. You weren't thinking about him when the maskless woman in the waiting room was telling you about her high hormone levels and empty sac, or when you were trying to read the book on your e-reader with the randomly inserted page numbers, or when you were having a piss, or picking a bit of sock fluff from between your toes, or replying to emails, or waiting for the traffic light to change, or kissing your partner good morning, or staring blankly out of the window while having your morning decaf tea and pretending it's a double espresso.

You were thinking about him, maybe, when you drove through an intersection and pictured a car smashing into the side of you. Not because he died like that, but because he died. You were thinking about him, maybe not the moment that you found out your partner had miscarried, the first or second or third time, but soon afterwards, because he died. You were thinking—

But now you're thinking about the intersection. Because the thing is, you can't drive. You wrote 'every time you drive through an intersection', but the actual truth, the thing you initially wrote and then deleted, is 'every time you're in the passenger seat of a car that someone else is driving through an intersection'. You deleted it because it feels clunky and draws attention to something that isn't important. It doesn't matter whether you're driving; it matters about the intersection, and how you imagine a car smashing into you. How often have you done this? In life and in writing? How often have you made the story tidier, made the truth say what you want it to say?

Often fiction sounds true and the truth sounds fake. There are things you know are true in a very dull and literal way, because they can be verified with documents and dates. Like the baby's due date. The baby, the only genetic heir in your immediate family, the only way the exact shade of your dad's eyes or the exact shape of his nose will ever exist on another human face. That baby being due a decade to the month since your dad died. It's ridiculous. It's too neat. You'd never write that in fiction. You'd never write that the nurse in the miscarriage room said she recognised you from a BBC ghost story reading you did, and you'd never write that you were recording another BBC ghost story the week your partner was getting the failed IVF. Ghosts at her first and last pregnancies. How cheap to bookend things like that, how false.

You've started crying at the end of yoga, like the worst kind of basic white girl. You can't help it; it's the affirmations. Today's was *you are doing your best*, and you just slumped in child's pose with tears dripping onto the carpet because you are trying your best at this, you really are, but still feel like you're doing a terrible job, like you're the world's worst pregnant person, that your partner was so much better at this, that everyone would prefer it if your partner was doing this and not you.

Pregnancy has made you feel more connected to your body: you love watching it grow and seeing what it can do, the power of it. But you feel disconnected from it too. Something is happening in your body that you can't see or control. You ask your body what's happening and it can't tell you. Is the baby alive, sleeping, healthy and happy, growing bigger every moment? Is it dead, hours dead, days dead, but you don't know it? Your body keeps its secrets.

Your first proper scan is next week. You have no bleeding. No strong pains. No lack of symptoms – they're stronger than ever. But your partner didn't have any bleeding or pains either. And still the baby was dead, and no one knew. You chair an online event for the British Library and the whole time you imagine yourself miscarrying. Are you bleeding onto your chair right now? It's a live event;

if you are miscarrying, should you just carry on, as there's nothing you can do anyway? Or should you unplug your wifi and pretend you've had a power cut? If you miscarry, how quickly will you be able to get pregnant again? If you try right away, are you really emotionally ready? But if you wait, will it be too late? And what if you miscarry again after that? What if your partner and you are both the 1 woman in 100 who has multiple miscarriages? It's unlikely. But when did being unlikely ever stop anything from happening?

You have your first midwife visit. She doesn't react when you use the 'she' pronoun for your partner. She asks you what your preferred pronouns are and notes it on the form. She asks about your medical history and your conception dates. She measures your weight and your blood pressure. The midwives work on a traffic light system and you're marked green for everything – except mental health, for which you're marked amber. You're almost thirty-eight and overweight and you've had multiple surgeries and all of that is fine. But your history of depression, self-harm and suicide attempt is not fine.

You wanted to get all green. You want the midwives to like you, to think that you're a good person, a good mother; worthy of this incredible fortune that's fallen on you. When your dad was dying you made sure to always be especially polite to the nurses. Not because you thought it was important to be nice to people, which you wish you could say was the case, but the truth is all you cared about was your dad and how much you didn't want him to die. You thought if you were nice to the nurses then they would think you were nice, and that your dad was nice, and so they'd treat him better, and so he wouldn't die. You thought that because your partner made the consultant laugh, they'd put the embryo in better, somehow, and the IVF would work. But no one is in control of this. No one at all.

You hear the amber as a judgement. You're not even a mother and you're already a terrible mother. The midwife tells you that the amber is just so everyone you see about the pregnancy knows to keep an eye on your mental health. It's to help them to support you. It's for your benefit. You don't believe her. You think they'll take the baby. You smile at her, trying to be good good good, trying to be nice nice nice, and you go home and you lie in bed and stare at the ceiling and worry.

It's the morning of the scan. You have cramps. Bad ones; period ones. Of course you would miscarry on the morning of the scan that would reassure you that you weren't going to miscarry. But when you go to the toilet, it's still great TP.

Your partner drives you to the hospital for the scan. A 90s station is playing on the radio. You know the words, but you don't sing along. There are so many intersections, and you brace yourself at each one.

Most of the couples in the waiting room appear to be male/female. There are two women together; you look at their body language while pretending you're looking at your phone. They don't kiss – but then no one kisses, everyone has a mask on. They don't seem like a couple. Friends? Sisters? We're all so early on in our pregnancies that it's impossible to tell which of us is pregnant. Your partner sits beside you, and you wonder if anyone can tell which of the two is pregnant. From the outside, it could be both. Or neither.

You're in the same scan room as when your partner had her missed miscarriage. The same bed. The same machine. The ghosts of you all in this room. You remember the too-short dress you were wearing that day. You remember the annoyed email you were writing in your head. You remember sitting in the plastic chair – the same one your partner is now sitting in. You remember the sound of your wail when they said there was no heartbeat. You remember the sonographer saying, *Get her out of here*; you don't know if this is an accurate memory. You remember sitting in the little beige room and crying so hard you choked and gasped like a baby. Aren't ghost stories fun? The same room. The same bed. It might even be the same sonographer. Get her out of here.

You smile at the sonographer even though she can't see through your mask. You lie up on the bed and roll your underwear down. Your hands start to shake; you hold them flat to your chest but it's still obvious. Tears leak from your eyes. You're not aware of crying, but the tears are there, falling into your ears. You say: *I'm sorry, I'm very nervous.* The sonographer replies cheerily, sympathetically, *First baby?* And you don't know how to answer. Yes. Not really. Yes, hopefully.

There we are! she says as a shape appears on the screen. You ask: *Is it okay? Is there a heartbeat?* An endless pause, in which your heart breaks, in which every plan you've made together shatters, in which all of this was for nothing.

Yes, she says. *There's a heartbeat.*

She says the baby is beautiful. She looks at the hands, the feet, the brain. You don't think you've ever been so relieved in your life. You keep saying, *Thank you, thank you.* You and your partner look at the baby arching its back and waving its hands. The sonographer presses hard on your belly, sweeps the scanner fast back and forth as if trying to erase pencil marks. There's a heartbeat. The baby is beautiful. It has hands and feet. There's a heartbeat.

The sun shines all week. You don't write anything and you don't care.

4

After the scan, a curtain lifts. The brain fog has gone. You don't feel randomly angry at certain foods. You can answer when your partner speaks to you. You clear your inbox. You call your accountant back. You negotiate a new home insurance deal. You read a book – and enjoy it. You write a new story. You think maybe it will be okay.

Everyone told you that after the first trimester, symptoms would reduce. They said a switch just flips. You thought, secretly, *That won't be me*. You thought you would be one of the rare ones who felt sick through the whole thing, or had a mass of complications, or had to be hospitalised. It always goes that way for you. You can't just have a sore back; you have to have a ruptured disc. You can't just have a headache; you have to have a rare form of migraine. *But there's nothing rare about this pregnancy*, your partner says. And she's right. She's the rare one, with her difficulty conceiving and multiple unexplained miscarriages. So far your conception and pregnancy have been absolutely textbook. Could it be that you will have a completely standard and complication-free pregnancy and birth, and yet be anxious and doom-laden for every day of it?

You're now further along than your partner's longest pregnancy. You both know it, but neither of you mentions it. You want to ask how she feels, but you can't bear to hear the answer. You don't know how you're both supposed to mourn the loss of one pregnancy journey while also celebrating the start of another. Grief and rejoicing. No life without death.

You're out on your own. She can't help you now. She couldn't really help you before, just like you couldn't help her when she was pregnant. But at least she could know in her body what you were feeling in yours. The sudden pains, the cravings, the exhaustion. Now you're in new territory. This strange new body. This strange new world. This strange new thing, alive inside you.

Your partner researches everything. Every spare moment is spent on her phone, looking at things. Cots. Car seats.

Rattles. Bibs. Babygrows. Baths. Bottles. What's the safest, what's the softest, what's the solidest, what's the best? This is how she feels in control. This is how she copes.

You cope by not letting her buy anything. She can research it and she can put in on a wish list, but she can't buy it. You have an image of the little sunshine-print babygrow, the woven Moses basket, the white-noise machine in the shape of a cloud, the ridiculous wooden toy espresso machine you've been coveting for months because it makes you imagine a weekend morning where you lie in bed in the bright new sun and your partner brings you a real flat white and your toddler brings you a pretend flat white and you express delight over both. You have an image of all these objects sitting in your flat after the baby dies. How cursed those things will be, how haunted.

You dream vividly every night. You dream that your mum buys a labyrinthine thirteen-bedroom apartment in Bucharest, entirely underground and windowless. That you're an alien changeling dropped into a family with many siblings, and you have to pass undetected even though you don't understand them or their ways.

Your bump pops. You look visibly pregnant, and you're only four months in. Every time you pass a mirror you look at your bump. You hold it. You rub it. You're glad your partner was at the scan so you can have reassurance you didn't imagine the whole thing. The thing about being a writer is that your inner life is as vivid as your outer life; sometimes you're not sure if something is real or only imagined, as both feel equally real to you. If you didn't know for sure you'd never been on a circus boat or an Arctic research station or the Middle Ages, like you've written about in your novels, you'd doubt your own life. Maybe that's why you write remote, fantastical things: so you can be sure you didn't live them.

You worry there is no baby. That you're just gaining weight because you've been eating more and barely exercising. That the baby belly you're lovingly stroking is just a belly. That you haven't had a period because there's something wrong with your insides. Your partner holds up the scan photo, asking, *Then what is this?*

So you watch your belly grow, your breasts. The skin is shiny and tight, your nipples huge and dark. Your belly is swollen from your ribs to a few inches below your belly button. You like watching it grow. It seems to get bigger every day. This is the first time in your adult life that you're seeing your body get bigger and being happy about it. The first time in your adult life that you don't think you need to be smaller. The first time in your adult life that you feel like your body looks exactly the way it's supposed to.

Your partner says your cunt smells sweet. You don't always call it that; for medical events it's a medical word (*when the sonographer put the probe in my vagina . . .*), when you have to be specific it's a specific word (*is that bit of blood on the toilet paper spotting, or do you have a scratch on your labia?*), when you're chatting it's a silly word (*this new underwear doesn't feel good on my fan-dan*). But when you speak of desire, it's always *cunt*. And your partner is right – your cunt does have a stronger smell in pregnancy. Even right after a shower you can smell it through your underwear if you squat down. It doesn't smell bad, just strong. Sweet. Pheromonal. Like you, and also like something new.

You masturbate when your partner is out at work. You do it quickly and efficiently, less than a minute from start to finish. You think of it as a medical process. Something you're doing to relax. It's self care. You do still worry that when you orgasm it will dislodge the baby. You read online that sex during pregnancy can be dangerous 'in rare circumstances'. But is the danger the orgasm, or the penetration? It doesn't say if masturbation carries the same danger. You also read, on a different website, that a mother's orgasm can be calming to the baby, as the walls of the uterus pulse soothingly, and of course the baby doesn't know what's going on. You choose to believe that instead.

You and your partner drive to the beach. You do this most weekends; both of you need regular top-ups of saltwater. It's a northern sort of landscape, just the type you like. The water pewter, choppy, wild. The silvered clouds and the gunmetal sea, pressing close. The smirr of rain kissing your cheeks. You wade in and stand with the waves enfolding your bare ankles, your belly held in your hands. You breathe deep, feeling the cold air stretch your lungs. You feel like a thing from the sea. You feel ancient, powerful, complete. *Are your feet cold?* your partner says. *Fucking freezing*, you say, and together you go back to the car.

Did you ever think, she says on the drive home, *that this baby will have six grandparents, but only be biologically related to one?* She's right: there's your mum, your stepdad, your partner's mum, your partner's stepdad, your partner's dad, your partner's stepmum. Six grandparents, and only one blood relative. No one has mentioned this, or seems to care. They're all too excited.

You were ready to be asked about the donor – even, ugh, the baby's 'father'. You had a series of responses prepared. To friends or family members, you'd simply say *a friend helped us*. To a queer woman who wanted tips on how to get pregnant herself, you'd share syringe recommendations and legal details. To a stranger, or someone you barely knew, just being nosy, you'd smile and tell them it's none of their business. You don't have to use any of these responses. The only person who asks is the midwife, and that's so she can fill in the form about any potential health problems for the baby. To your great surprise, no one else asks. Not strangers, not friends. Even your partner's plethora of very close, very chatty aunts. As far as everyone around you seems to be concerned, the only people involved in this baby are you and your partner.

You want to swim, but you worry. You worry about how you'll look in your swimsuit. You worry the pool will be too busy. You worry you'll get accidentally kicked in the belly. You worry you're so enormous you won't be able to actually swim, just float around like a manatee. You go anyway.

It's a rainy day and the outdoor pool is empty. Dead leaves float on the surface. The wind kicks the water into ripples. Any sensible person would swim in the indoor pool, which is warmer and brighter and cleaner. But you want, more than anything, to lie in the water and look up at the sky. The second you get in the pool, your brainwaves change to something slower, longer, looser. Your brain quietens. You take a breath and drop beneath the water. You float. You stretch your limbs, your hands and feet, feeling the bones crack and joints shift. You feel the rain patter on the surface above you. You let the water hold you. You let your body hold the baby.

5

You ask on Twitter for recommendations of books on pregnancy and motherhood – you don't want guides, you say, but literary books, memoirs, essays. A stranger responds that when she was pregnant she didn't read any books, she *just winged it*. She asks you: *Afraid?* You draft several responses to her – jaunty responses, indignant responses, haughty responses, sympathy-demanding responses. You delete them all. You wonder if this woman goes up to pregnant strangers in the street, to people pushing babies in buggies, and asks if they're afraid. You wonder if they reply.

What a stupid question. Of course you're afraid.

You still struggle to say the phrase *I'm pregnant*. You don't like the pronoun. You don't like this description of yourself. It doesn't feel yours to own. You don't think of yourself as someone who is pregnant. The closest you can come is, *My partner and I are expecting a baby*. It's not wrong; you and your partner have been expecting to have a baby for several years.

But it's not entirely accurate either. You've given up on expecting. All you dare do is hope.

Your pregnancy is now viable. If something goes wrong and the baby dies inside you, it's called a stillbirth, not a miscarriage. But if something goes wrong and they can get the baby out, there's a chance it will live on its own. You cling to that thought. You still check the toilet paper for blood, calling out *great TP!* to your partner. You still picture yourself leaving a trail of blood behind you in the swimming pool. You still worry about crashing the car or falling in the shower. Slipping between the train carriage and the platform. Being knifed by a stranger. Tripping onto a carving knife. Getting attacked by wild dogs. Being crushed by scaffolding. Your body, out of control. Your insides, outside.

Your anxiety never gets to resolve. You can't fight it or flee from it, because there's nothing there. It just loops and loops and loops, over and over and over.

Everyone tells you to sleep now, as you won't get any sleep when the baby arrives. You try, but your body says otherwise. You wake every night at 3 a.m. and can't get back to sleep. Nothing works. Not the plane crash podcast. Not your partner stroking your hair. Not an orgasm. You get up, make tea and sit on the couch by the window. There's a book in your lap, but you don't read it. In the flats around you, every window is dark. The roads are silent. You listen to your own breathing. You watch the dried grasses in a vase on the windowsill shiver in the breeze. A fox flits across the road. It feels like being in on a secret. You wonder if this is what if will feel like to wake in the night and feed the baby, rock the baby, soothe the baby, sing to the baby. You wonder if there will be a baby. You wonder if instead you will wake in the night on the baby's due date, your belly empty, the cot empty, rocking a ghost.

You're still convinced that the baby will die. You were sure you would miscarry. Now you're sure you'll have a stillbirth. Or the baby might die of cot death a few days or weeks after birth. You can't imagine the baby any older than a few weeks. You find it hard to imagine any possibility that doesn't include the baby dying. You're already making plans for when and if you could try again. If your body and mind could handle it, and how soon. You wasted so much time before starting to try. You couldn't have done this any sooner, but you wish you had anyway.

Here's what you want: a white room. A bed with white sheets. White curtains wafting in the breeze from the open window. The type of hospital room you've never seen in real life, but that feels familiar from movies. You want a kind but stern nurse who will pad around in soft-soled shoes and inject you with something without telling you what it is. Some kind of medium-strength painkillers so you can drift, not quite awake and not quite asleep. You want to stay in that bed, drifting, floating, weightless, worryless, through this whole pregnancy. You want them to wake you when it's all over and put the baby in your arms and tell you it's all okay. See? It was always going to be okay.

You remember your dad in various rehabs and psychiatric residences, and just for a moment you envy that, you want that, the simplicity of it, the single-mindedness.

You try not to look at mummy social media, but it creeps in. You know it's toxic, but you keep going back to it, the way you eat cheap chocolate even though it makes your teeth feel furry and your blood sugar hum and you keep eating it beyond the point of enjoying the taste. The social media mums say their (male, always male) partners are jealous of the baby and the attention it consumes. They resent the domestic confinement. They chafe against their new role as parent. They are disappointed that their sexy, groomed wives are now covered in old milk and vomit.

They're bored of nappies and feeding and night waking. You wonder how much of this will affect your partner, if any. Will you be the resentful one? Will you be jealous, chafing, disappointed? You're the more traditionally masculine one, after all. You might appear to be more traditionally feminine: you have longer hair and wear make-up and dresses; more importantly, perhaps, you're the pregnant one. But she's more naturally maternal. She's nurturing, caring, patient, kind – all of the things you're not, or that you try to be, but often fail.

Have you felt any kicks? your partner asks hesitantly one night. *No*, you say, *not yet. Maybe?* Because you don't know what a baby moving inside you is meant to feel like. You lie in bed, your partner resting her hand on your belly as she does every night, and she googles it. *It should feel like bubbles*, she says. *Like a butterfly's wings fluttering. Like a tiny fish swimming.* That seems deeply unhelpful to you; how are you meant to know what it feels like to have a tiny fish swimming inside you? *I don't feel a fish*, you say. *Do you feel a fish?* Your partner takes her hand away. *I wouldn't feel it anyway*, she says. *Not from the outside.*

After you got married, you honeymooned in Iceland. You understood that most people go to hot places, beaches, sunshine; but you're both north people. You like snow and ice, a wild sea, a whipping wind, cosying in by the fire under the vast black sky. When you were driving around in the early dark, trying to find your remote cabin, your partner pointed out a faint flicker in the sky. *Northern lights*, she said. *Can't be*, you replied. *It's just the Reykjavik city lights, or a searchlight from the airport.* You'd seen photos of the northern lights; those flows and twists of green-purple-pink, vivid as tropical fish, bright as neon. These lights didn't look like that; they were much fainter and subtler. You could only glimpse them from the corner of your eye. If you tried to catch them, there was nothing there. *No*, your partner insisted, *it is the northern lights*. She stopped the car and you both got out, lying back on the car bonnet, bundled up in your fur-hooded coats, boots on the black earth. You watched and waited. And she was right. It was the northern lights. They'd been there the whole time, as you'd been looking and not seeing.

I keep feeling like I need to fart, you say to your partner. *My guts move around, but then no fart comes. Does the website say it can feel like that?* She consults her phone. *They mostly say fish or butterflies or bubbles*, she says. *But this one says it can feel like indigestion?* You grab her hand and press it to your belly. *That's what I feel!* you say. You've also had indigestion and heartburn and nausea most days, but still. You really, really want this to be a kick. *It must be it,* you say. *Can you feel it?* She holds her hand very still. She barely breathes. She listens with her hand. *I'm not sure*, she says. *Neither am I*, you say.

Your partner reads on the internet that the baby can see light now, so you decide to do a baby disco: you sweep her phone torch across your belly while she sings and plays guitar. Abba, The Supremes, First Aid Kit. You can't pinpoint the exact moment you feel the baby moving; it's not a sudden shift, more of a slow understanding. The baby kicks the most when your partner sings, when you're lying in bed, the vast island of you on your ever-growing mass of pillows, cradling your belly, half-dozing, drunk on your own happiness. *The baby either loves it and is dancing around*, your partner says, *or hates it and is trying to get me to stop*. You love that the baby is already familiar with her voice. The baby doesn't even know the world outside exists, but still knows that your partner's voice is in it.

Your partner confesses to you that she finds the baby's kicks exciting, but also terrifying. With every passing day, the pregnancy gets safer, the baby stronger. But with every passing day, you love the baby more, and feel a stronger fear that it will all be taken away. The missed miscarriage, the early bleeds, the failed promise of the IVF: for both of you, the only experiences with pregnancy before this have been bad. You have nothing else to compare it to. You have no other model for what to expect.

You want to be careless with your pregnancy. You want to say: *Oh go on, I'll have some soft cheese, I'll have a sip of wine, I'll have an espresso. Why the hell not?* You want to believe, as you used to, that a pregnancy meant a baby. You want to take it for granted; you want to forget. But you're never not thinking about it.

One night, baby disco starts as usual. You settle back on your pillow mound and cup your belly in your hands. *I was thinking Ane Brun tonight*, your partner says, and starts singing. But you feel nothing. No kicks. No flutters. You wait until the end of the song, but still nothing. Instantly you're in a state of worry. It's not true to say you worry: your entire state changes. You are transported to an entirely different place, and it's called Worry, and you don't know the way back.

Your partner phones the midwife. Her tone soft, she calls you both honey and sweetie and tells you not to worry, that at this stage it doesn't count as decreased movement, that the baby is still so small and has so much room to move that it can get into strange positions so you can't feel it. *I'm sure it's fine*, you say to your partner. You know she has to get up early for work, and there's nothing either of you can do anyway. *Let's just go to sleep*, you say. You lie awake all night, hands pressed to your belly, barely moving, barely breathing, praying to no one, desperate to feel something.

At 6 a.m., you feel a series of flicks low on your left side, by your hip bone. That can't be the baby. It can't be that far round. You wake your partner up in a panic at 7 a.m. By then you've already imagined everything that could go wrong; the exact words you'd use to tell people the baby has died; whether you could bear to ever try again; whether that will become your story now: the two queer women who should never have tried to have a baby in the first place.

Your partner holds you and makes you breathe. You read on the internet that moving around, eating, talking to the baby can make them move so you get up and make tea, drink it calmly while rubbing your belly. You feel a flicker. Then another. It must be your guts, your heartbeat stuttering; you won't believe it's the baby until you get one good, solid kick. Just one. Please, just one. The flickers increase and move. As you're sobbing onto your partner's shoulder and she's telling you, *I've found a place that does private scans and has appointments in an hour, we can go straight away and wait outside until it opens, just put a jumper on and get in the car, we can go right now* – that's when you get it: a good, solid kick. Then another. The baby is there. Alive.

It's your partner's forty-first birthday. Glasgow is still locked down so you take her to a nice hotel ten minutes up the road. It's a spaceship-like pod room, and the shower has translucent walls. You soak under the hot water and your partner takes a photo of you through the translucent wall, lit by pink lights, bump protruding. You go out for pizza, then watch films in the white-sheeted bed. You fall asleep almost instantly. The bed is huge, the room is warm, and all three of you sleep late.

6

You're thinking about hauntings. You're thinking about the baby, as you're always thinking about the baby. You are possessed by the baby.

But you possess the baby too. You have a skeleton within your skeleton. Your body has made a whole new body.

And your body isn't stopping at the necessary parts. You were an overachiever with piss – now you're an overachiever with skin. You've had maybe one skin tag in your entire life but now, suddenly, you have several, at the places where your body meets itself: in your armpits, at your crotch. You have to navigate them when you shave so you don't cut them off. All these excess bits, as if your body, thrilled at what it can create, got carried away and kept making things.

You think about the skin tag bit while brushing your teeth before bed. You wander to the kitchen, to the table where you write, and open the laptop. You type in the dark by the laptop's glow, toothbrush hanging out of your mouth. Your partner comes in to see what you're doing, murmurs to herself, *The book*, then walks out again. She doesn't know which book it is, and you don't suppose it matters. That's how you know she's been married to a writer for a while; this random drifting-aside doesn't seem strange to her any more.

You've reached the 'shoplifting a honeydew' stage of pregnancy. You walk around holding your belly with both hands like a sack of flour. You groan when you stand up. Your feet puff up like bread rolls if you're upright for more than a few minutes. You've heard from friends that when they were visibly pregnant, everyone felt a kind of ownership; even strangers came up to them and, unasked, touched their belly. But not you. You float like a manatee in the outdoor pool. You take up a whole aisle in the supermarket, cutting through like a vast galleon, belly first, a ship's figurehead. You wander stacks in the library, flipping through a book that rests on the swell of you. You move through the world, vast and untouched.

There's one benefit of being pregnant during a pandemic: no touching.

You meet your partner's friend for brunch. She brings her six-month-old baby, who is a delight, as is the friend. But you're hormonal and exhausted and you do not charm the friend. You do not charm the baby either. You hold him, but you don't know what to do. He chews his fist and looks expectantly at you. You don't know what he wants, and suddenly he arches his back, making it impossible for you to hold him. You worry he's going to hit his head on the table or scald himself on a flat white. You can't give him any baby toys to play with as you didn't bring any – you don't even have any baby toys; you've refused to let your partner buy anything, no cot, no pram, no clothes, no toys. You keep saying: *Let's just wait. Let's just check everything is okay.* You jangle your keys for the baby, making sure to keep them out of his reach. He fidgets and whines, as if he senses your desperation. You feel like everyone in the café is watching you struggle with this baby, then looking at your enormous bump and thinking how shit you'll be as a mother. Not even a mother yet, and already you've failed at it.

You read books about motherhood. Dozens of them. You've been collecting them for years, ever since you and your partner started trying for a baby, but you could never bring yourself to read them, too distracted by your envy. But now you don't need to be envious; you're like them. You read about women who ache and scream for some time alone, then when they get it they do nothing but moon over the baby until they are reunited. You read about women who go outside as their children nap and crouch behind the garage, woodlice tickling their ankles, the stink of the bins, so desperate are they to be alone. You read about women who have wanted to write a novel, a short story, a single haiku for several years but never get to have a clear thought, never mind write anything down. You read about motherhood as a relentless, thankless slog. As ceaseless labour. As a silent scream. As a rage that burns inside and must be tamped down, down, down, it's okay, Mummy's fine, it didn't even hurt, it wasn't valuable, I didn't want it anyway. As a requirement to abandon all your dreams. As a requirement to deny your own desires. As a requirement to ignore your own wellbeing. As sacrifice after sacrifice after sacrifice.

You put down the books and pick up your phone. Your phone, of course, knows you're pregnant, so you immediately fall into a pit of targeted content. You scroll through 'relatable' social media posts about being reduced to an exhausted milk bag that children trample on, grab for, poke in the eye, and who no one respects or desires any more, remember when I used to have a career, remember when I spoke to grown-ups, why can't my husband even unload a dishwasher, why do my kids throw food in my face and then laugh, haha, relatable, #justmomthings. You don't want that life. But maybe that's the life you've already chosen and you don't know it yet. Maybe an anvil is about to fall on your head, and you know it, and you don't dare look up.

You're determined that baby brain won't happen to you. You had enough in the first trimester; you've paid your dues. But you feel yourself get clumsy, unwieldy. You struggle for words. You feel like all your thoughts are on a long slow loop. You're awake, aware – but just there. Like a mannequin. Like you're on pause. You chip two plates within a few minutes. You cut your finger on a tin and have to go to minor injuries to get butterfly stitches. The next day you slam the bandaged finger in a drawer, rip off the stitches, and have to go back and get them done again. When you turn up at the same clinic, with the same finger wrapped in a bloody tea towel, of course it would be the same nurse at reception. You laugh at yourself, haha, relatable, #justmomthings. You drop your phone on the floor in the waiting room and try not to let anyone see that you cracked the screen. Later, taking your dinner out of the oven, you burn your wrist and drop half the food on the floor. You put it in the dog's bowl and don't allow yourself to cry. You're fine. You're still the same person you were before the pregnancy. You're not like every other pregnant person in the world. You're different, somehow. You're #notlikeothermoms.

You go back to your shelf of motherhood books. You read about how motherhood is awful, a drudge, about how you have no time, no thoughts, it's all just red jellyfish brain and rage but nowhere to put it so you just float, wordless, meaningless. You'll never have time again. You'll never think again.

But. You read this in a book, didn't you? A book written by a mother. The book is intelligent, insightful, surprising. The book makes you envious; you wish you could write such beautiful prose, could have such insight. All these books were written by people with babies.

You look at the shelf, the whole shelf of books about motherhood written by mothers. You rub the bandage on your finger, feeling the skin underneath healing.

7

Your mum speculates about the baby. She says: *You have blue eyes, and your partner has brown eyes, so the baby's eyes could be either.* Your partner's mum says: *You'd better watch out, she was walking at six months old, so you'll have an early mover on your hands.* You've all started doing it: speaking of your partner as the other biological parent. Then there's a pause, as you remember.

You and your partner go out for brunch with your donor and his partner. Your partner sits by his partner, and you sit by him. They're your close friends, and you see them often, but this feels different. Due to the ever-shifting rules of the pandemic lockdown, and your terror of getting Covid while pregnant, for months you've only seen them in your flat. Now here you are, all in public together. Your bump is undeniable, pressing against the table. You like being visibly pregnant, but you don't like that it often makes people assume you're heterosexual. You think you read as queer, but only borderline queer. Your short, blunt-chopped hair with an undercut, dyed an unnatural colour; the bright tattoos on your arms; your little pin badges with sassy slogans on them. It's all just costuming – but it's your costume. It's your book cover, explaining what's inside. Other queer people will probably read you correctly, but you can pass undetected in the straight world. Yet pregnancy has tipped you into reading as straight. And now here you are, having brunch with a man, your big baby belly out and proud. You know that it appears as if he's the baby's father. Which, in a traditional sense, he is. But also, according to you and your partner and him and his partner and all of your families and friends, is very much not.

Coming out isn't a one-time thing. You don't tell someone – or even everyone – that you're queer and then that's it for ever, it's branded on your forehead and you need never explain it again. You have to come out every day. Every time someone asks about your partner and you have to correct the pronoun. Every time you answer a question about the baby's 'father'. Every time, you have to make a choice: do you correct and clarify, or do you slip by, invisible?

You've long considered yourself outside the male gaze. You're not interested in men in that way, and haven't been for years. Whether men – all men, or specific men – find you attractive is irrelevant to your life. You don't care what men think about how you dress, act, speak, fuck, or do basically anything. Your queerness puts you at one remove from the male gaze – being visibly queer means that men simply don't look at you as much. Your age is another – now you're thirty-eight, men don't look at you like they did in your twenties. Being pregnant puts you at another remove. But you've started to notice other women looking at you. Not with desire, but with interest, usually women who are also pregnant or pushing buggies. Sometimes they smile. Sometimes they just acknowledge you. It reminds you of the way that two visibly queer women will acknowledge one another in the street.

Your partner has been on the internet again. *I think we should try perineal massage*, she says. She's bought a tiny bottle of oil specifically for this purpose. You examine the bottle. You know your partner is feeling bad about going back to work after the summer holiday. She wants to be here, making all your meals, making sure you don't climb any ladders, arranging the cushions under your puffy feet, driving you to the swimming pool so you can do your laps in the rain, feeling the baby kick any time she wants. She wants to be needed. She wants to be vital to this process.

She knows you're terrified of tearing during the birth, and she's doing what she can to mitigate that fear. *I love massage*, you say, and resume your usual evening position on your throne of pillows. Perineal massage sounds sexy to you. Medical, but also sexy. Lube, your cunt, your partner's fingers. You've been here before, and it was pretty sexy then. *It reduces the chances of perineal trauma during birth*, she reads from the instructions. *The aim*, she continues, *is to use two fingers to stretch the area of skin and muscle between the vagina and anus*. Words like 'stretch' and 'trauma' should clue you in to what's about to happen, but you're still hung up on the word 'massage'. Massage is pleasant. Relaxing. Enjoyable. *What's not to like?* you say.

Your partner slips her thumbs inside you, then presses them gently against the back wall of your vagina. *The instructions say I should hold it for two minutes, and you should feel a bit of a stretching feeling*, she says. *Do you feel it?* You don't feel anything much. She's being too hesitant. You know it won't work if you don't feel it. *You have to do it a bit more*, you say, and she does, just a tiny bit, a millimetre more, and you hear yourself cough out, *What the fuck*.

It is not a stretching feeling. It is a horrible aching burning feeling. It feels like someone is uncomfortably stretching your genitals, which is exactly what it is. She asks if you can feel it now and all you can do is grimace. *The instructions say that you'll get used to the burning sensation*, she says. *That it's not pain, only stretching.* You try not to move, but your entire body wants to leap away from her and run out of the room. *I really feel like*, you say, *it can be both at once.* You know there's going to be a lot more pain and a lot more stretching in labour, and you're pissed that you don't even get a reprieve until then. It has to be lots of smaller stretches as well as the massive big one. *Do you want me to stop?* your partner says. *Now I'm meant to massage the lower bit of your vagina for around two to three minutes.* Of course you want her to stop. You don't want your perineum stretched. You don't want anyone pressing against the back wall of your vagina. But you also don't want to tear during birth. *No,* you say, in the saddest and angriest voice you've ever used. *Keep going.* You hold your body motionless, letting the rage emanate from you.

Well, you say, lying back on your pillows, vagina mercifully empty. *Turns out there's a lot not to like.* And you have to do it all again tomorrow. *I can't believe they have the cheek to call it massage*, your partner says. *They should call it perineal torture*, you say. *But then*, she says, *possibly fewer people would do it.*

You're afraid of being alone, suddenly. You've always loved being alone. You work at home alone all day and have done for years. You go for writing residencies for a week or a month, all alone. You eat in restaurants alone, browse in bookshops alone, go for walks alone. You love the company of your friends and family but you don't need it, don't feel lost and lonely without it; you're only around people when you want to be. But now it terrifies you. You need someone else there to check on reality. Because what if you're imagining it all? What if the baby doesn't really move, and what you think is movement is actually nothing at all? *Look*, you say: *look at my belly! Look at it roll, look the kicks!* And your mum, or your friend, who has already seen and felt your belly move a dozen times, smiles and says, *Yes, I see it*. Your partner is the only other person who, like you, is content to just sit and watch your skin bulge and pulse. Every night when you go to sleep, your partner puts her hands on your belly. You fall asleep almost instantly, knowing that you've handed the baby off to someone else to watch over. The baby is real. You're not imagining it.

The perineal massage gets easier. Your partner says she can feel the difference. Perhaps it's just that you're more relaxed, or perhaps your vagina really is getting more elastic. You're not sure how you feel about having an elasticated vagina. Every time she does the massage, your partner insists on using her phone torch so she can properly see what she's doing. But she knows that whole area perfectly well; she's not going to get lost. She's just fascinated by it. The swollen pink labia. The visible clitoris pouting out. You haven't seen your pubic area for many months now, so she helps you shave (and cut your toenails, and put on your socks, and do anything else that your belly gets in the way of). Although you can't see it, you're also fascinated. You can feel your labia all the time. They're puffy, blood-swollen, like the tip of a finger if you tied a thread around it.

You've been thinking about how you are a creature inside which something moves. About monsters and wonders. Selkies. Kelpies. Mermaids. Sirens, serpents, krakens. The Loch Ness Monster. Things beautiful and terrifying that lurk in the dark waters. You've written about sea creatures over and over in your stories. Why do you keep diving down to them? What is it down there that fascinates you? You've written also about your fear of pregnancy, of having something hidden and growing inside you. Something writhing and gnashing, roiling in the black waters.

But the water soothes you even as it scares you. Perhaps that's the draw of things: repulsion and desire, all at once. You're still swimming in the outdoor pool every week. As you float you imagine the baby floating too; this is when you feel most connected. Your mother-in-law told you that when she was pregnant with your partner, she was most active in the bath. She's not usually sentimental, your affectionate but practical mother-in-law, but when she speaks of this it's in loving descriptions of lying in the warm water, resting her hands on the island of her belly, watching it roll. For you, it's the opposite. Every time you swim, the baby sleeps through it all. So calm, your water baby. Your selkie, your kraken. A monster and a wonder.

8

You've written about your fear of enclosed spaces. You've tried to exorcise it in stories many times. You've written about a woman bricking herself up in a wall, about a woman who won't remove the doll's house from her head, about a woman living in a spite house so small her outstretched hands could touch both walls, about a woman and a bear who live on a tiny coracle on the endless ocean, about a woman and her mermaid lover on a small island, about a group of people trapped and haunted in an Arctic base. You're struggling to think of a setting you've ever imagined, over a decade of writing and millions of words, that isn't enclosed in some way. You're eight months pregnant. The baby is the size of a squash. The baby is the weight of a joint of beef. You google illustrations of babies in utero at eight months, and you can't bear to look. You close the tab so you don't accidentally see it the next time you look at your phone. But it's not enough; you have to put your phone away, as if to exorcise the idea. The baby can barely move. The baby can't see. The baby is in a dim underwater cave, trapped motionless in the dark. The baby is in words like crepuscular, tenebrous, stygian; the baby is in a Gothic horror.

You discuss these things with your partner as you promenade slowly around the park, avoiding the hills, circling the duck pond. It's an unseasonably cool day and you're wearing a scarf. When you glance down at your body, it's shapeless, unknowable; all you see is the scarf. You get the feeling you've forgotten something and pat your pockets to check. Keys, phone, mask. That's all you need. So why do you still feel like you forgot something? You look down at your body. At your scarf. Shit, you think, you forgot your bump.

You realise your partner is saying something. *But*, she says, *the baby doesn't know claustrophobia. The baby doesn't know anything outside your body*. It's more than that: the baby doesn't know there even is anything outside your body. Your body, as far as the baby is concerned, is the whole world.

You don't want to start writing anything new, but you can think about it. You've always thought of writing as a process of going inside. Inside a house, inside a world, inside yourself. You go in and shut the door, and that's where the story lives. When you're writing, as your partner has often pointed out, you have no awareness of what's happening around you. You don't see or hear things; you can even give vague responses to questions, and then have no memory that you spoke. Everything you're currently interested in is inside you: the baby in your body, the stories in your mind. You like that you're all in there together: you, the baby, the stories. You can hold everything inside you.

You're almost there. In the home stretch. The baby has moved down, shifted into place. You can breathe. You feel tiny kicks in your ribs, a headbutt deep inside. You feel content. Slow, satisfied. The baby could come any day, any time, in the next two months. Here's another thing you never knew before getting pregnant: it doesn't last for nine months. Pregnancy is forty weeks, which is almost ten months, and you're allowed to go two weeks overdue before you're induced. It's like a corridor in a dream: you think you've reached the end, but every time you get closer the end stretches further and further away. Every day feels like the last, like something precious and final, something that needs to be commemorated. Perhaps today is the baby's birthday. No: perhaps tomorrow. No? The next day, then. There's no point in starting anything, as it could be abandoned at any moment; but also two months is a lot of time. You allow yourself to sit and rest. You feel yourself thicken and sweeten, like milk turning to cream.

Before being pregnant you never asked your mum about your own birth. You had little curiosity about her pregnancy with you – how long it took, how she felt, what went right and what went wrong. Now you know all about it, and her pregnancy with your brother, and your mother-in-law's pregnancies with both of her children, and your sister-in-law's pregnancies with both hers. Even your friends' pregnancies and births, which you'd never thought to ask about before, thinking that it wasn't for you to ask about, it was their private business, as all medical things are. Now you know all about them, and could know even more if you delved deeper; absolutely no one you speak to is reluctant to talk about their own pregnancy and birth; they seem thrilled, in fact, to speak again about it.

You've often heard people say, wonderingly and indignantly, that there aren't any books on motherhood. That no one is talking about it. That it's ignored and silenced due to, probably, the patriarchy. You're not so sure about this. Not about the patriarchy, which you won't defend, but about the silence. You've read dozens of books on conception, pregnancy and parenthood; queer experiences, trans and nonbinary experiences, joyful experiences, disappointing experiences, spiritually transcendent experiences, savage and brutal experiences. You think, actually, lots of people are talking about this. Hollie McNish, Doireann Ní Ghríofa, Chitra Ramaswamy, Erica Gillingham, Jenn Ashworth, Anne Lamott, Rachel Cusk, Sinéad Gleeson, Candice Brathwaite, Rivka Galchen, Louise Erdrich, Laura Dockrill, Maggie Nelson, Charlotte Runcie. They're all talking about it. Perhaps the thing is that the people who say no one is talking aren't actually listening? You know that before your own pregnancy, you weren't listening. You're finding it incredible, now, to hear all these new voices, and annoyed at yourself that you didn't listen before.

You didn't know that the baby's first movements would feel like you were about to fart, and that you would only know it was actually the baby because no fart would come. You didn't know your nipples would start tingling and itching like they'd been stung by nettles as your milk ducts opened. You didn't know your labia would swell, your clitoris pout. You could have probably learned these things by reading books by other people who had gone through the same experience. But you didn't read those books, because you were afraid. You were afraid of pregnancy and afraid of birth, and you thought if you learned too much about it then you wouldn't want to do it.

That's not true. Not entirely. You didn't read those books because those books were all by people who had babies. Living, healthy babies. You knew there was a baby, because that's why a book about babies was written, and you envied them that inevitability. No one in these books seemed to be terrified that their baby was going to die. Perhaps they were, but the books don't say so. Why, you think, did no one tell me?

Still, you wrote so often about pregnancy and motherhood, long before you knew anything about them. Something drew you to the subject long before you had any interest in being pregnant. All those words you wrote. So many of them about pregnancy loss and death. Babies dying in the womb. Children drowning in the sea. Children dying of starvation or cold. What did you know about it then? What do you know about it now? Such authority you claimed. You made babies in books knowing you were going to kill them. Making them purely so that you could kill them. Why did you do that? Did you think it was sadder? Yes. It was sad. And that's why you wrote it.

Every day you break down in panicked tears because you're terrified of stillbirth. Sometimes it's all you can think about. You can imagine it all so vividly, even when you try not to. You try to distract yourself with work, emails, making plans for future books. You try going out for lunch with friends, browsing at the library, binge-watching complex crime dramas while bouncing on your yoga ball. But through all of it you feel the panic just beneath the surface. If you stop moving for too long then the tears will seep out, your breath will start to come fast, your knees will start to bounce in panic. What if you've done all this for nothing? What if this was all just a trick? What if the thing you finally allowed yourself to believe was real isn't real at all? You spend hours on the internet looking up stillbirth statistics to convince yourself how unlikely it is. Your partner comes home and finds you in a panic, doom-scrolling. *The baby has been fine so far*, she says, *and it'll most likely continue to be fine.* You want to be comforted by her but you just cry and say, *But you don't know, no one knows.*

You're almost due. The midwife asks about your birth plan, and you don't know how to tell her that you don't have one, because you can't bear to think about the birth. Labour doesn't sound so bad to you. Just the end part. You don't fear pain; you fear damage. You're not worried about the contractions; only the ripping or the cutting, the image of all your insides being forced out of you. You still don't know what to tell them. You don't know much about mother-hood, but already you do know that whatever you plan for doesn't happen. You expected for your partner to carry the child; her body wouldn't comply. You expected that you'd carry reluctantly, hating every moment; you're ending up enjoying pregnancy, even loving it. You expect that you'll miscarry, that you'll have a stillbirth, that blood will stain your seat every time you stand; you seem to be having a textbook pregnancy with no problems. You've avoided pre-eclampsia, diabetes, placenta previa. The baby's heartbeat is – and always has been – strong, the movements good and regular, everything normal and boring and typical, just the way you wanted. Everyone tells you to make a birth plan, then throw it away. That seems like a waste of time to you, but it's what you've been told to do, so you do it.

A water birth, you say to your partner, who is filling in the birth plan template she downloaded from the NHS website. You're thinking about your hours in the outdoor pool, your trips to the sea. *Will you want a beanbag?* your partner asks. *Will you want any mats? Will you want to be in bed with your back propped up with pillows? Would you like to squat? Would you like a TENS machine?* You don't know. You don't know any of this. How can you possibly know?

All you can focus on is what you do know. Your due date is tomorrow. In the past few days, your nipples no longer secrete golden flecks of colostrum. All your skin tags have fallen off. Your body is shedding what it doesn't need, readying itself for birth. The baby is moving. You feel healthy. Everything is fine. Everything is fine. Please, God I don't believe in, let everything be fine, please please please.

You swim fifty lengths in the outdoor pool, practising your labour breathing, pushing dead leaves aside with your prayered hands as you breaststroke. As you swim you imagine being in labour. You tip your head back and let the soft rain fall on your face. You sink below the surface, your eyes shut against the water, your ears hearing nothing but the muffled thud of your own heart. Now you hear what the baby hears. Now you feel what the baby feels. You let the water hold you. You try to pin it all in your mind; you imagine that during labour you'll go to this place and find peace.

9

The baby is almost two weeks overdue. You're scheduled in for induction, though you still hope the baby will make an appearance before it's needed. You get your bloody show and your mucus plug. You and your partner are both obsessed with the things that come out of you. *Come and see!* you shout from the bathroom when you wipe and find a glob of Vaseline-like goo, pale pink with blood. *It's great TP!* you add, before she thinks the worst. You save the blood and mucus wrapped up in toilet paper, just in case you need to show someone. Your cunt smells strange and sweet, like molasses. You think of the novel you wrote about a woman and a bear living in a coracle. You love that word, coracle. You picture your hips as a coracle of bone, holding the baby, floating on the night-time sea.

You think of a story you wrote about a theatre with very long red velvet curtains that would open with much effort and a slow sweeping swish. You picture your cervix as a dark red curtain, slowly pulling back.

You cuddle up to your partner and she rests her hands on your bump, as she does every night. You think about how in love you both are. How you're both so wildly in love with someone you've never met, whose face you've never seen, whose voice you've never heard. You would both do anything for someone you don't know.

Your dreams have become so literal. After packing your hospital bag, you dream you're late and frantically packing for a flight, but can't find anything.

You have been pregnant for so long. You have been pregnant for years. You have never not been pregnant. Everyone you see – your mum, your mother-in-law, your friends, your great-aunt, the cleaners at your partner's work, the woman in the café, the staff in the pharmacy, asks: *No baby yet?* You reply cheerfully, *Not yet!* You feel blamed. Everyone wants to meet the baby, and it's your fault they can't. You're selfish, keeping the baby all to yourself; you're lazy, not wanting to go through the birth. But you want to have the baby. You're ready. You don't care if it hurts. You don't care how long it takes. When people say, *No baby yet,* you hear: *Why can't you do this? What's wrong with you?*

This is the biggest you've ever been. You spent most of your teens and twenties slim without trying, and after you met your partner at twenty-nine you gradually gained weight. The week you met her, you wrote in your journal: 'she will make me fat and happy'. And she did. In your thirties your metabolism slowed, you filled yourself up on your partner's cooking; you cared more about what your body could do than how it looked. You made your peace with it, its possibilities and its limitations. But you go back and forth on this. Some days you look in the mirror with horror, not recognising who you've become. What you've become. But most days you love your new body: your growing bump, your dimpled thighs, your blue-veined breasts, your creased neck, your swollen ankles, your swaying upper arms. Perhaps because you still believe this is a temporary state, a costume you're trying on; after, you can go back to your previous body, put it back on like a too-small dress hidden at the back of the wardrobe.

A part of you knows that you can't go back. Your feet, your wrists, your gums, your hairline, your nipples, your armpits, your blood. There's not a single part of your body, inside or outside, that hasn't been changed. You have the baby's cells inside you, and they will stay there for decades. Your body will never be entirely your own again.

You wake from a nap on the sofa, your partner stroking your hair, and hear a lowing noise, like a cow, coming from the TV. Your partner is watching a programme about birth. She's watched a dozen of these; she's seen literally hundreds of births. But you won't watch a single episode. You can't even think about it. The woman on the TV is huge, unwieldy, bellowing like an animal. You don't have your glasses on, so the screen is blurry. You see what looks like meat, blood, purplish innards, organs and cords thick with gristle. The woman screams and moans. She's saying something but it's impossible to tell what. Maybe she doesn't even know what. *Please switch it off*, you say. She switches it off. You can't bear how out of control it all seems, how animalistic. Will that be you? How could that be you?

You know what I learned today? your partner says, her voice very soft, very soothing. She strokes your hair back from your forehead as she speaks. *It's the baby, not your body, that starts labour. It releases a hormone when it's ready to come out. The baby is in control, and your body just responds.*

So that's what you will do, you tell yourself. You will give yourself over to the baby. You will let the baby be in control. Come on, baby. Let's do this together.

You ask your partner: *Will you still be able to look at my cunt with desire after you've seen a baby come out of it? After you've seen it split open, bloody, and possibly with shit on it?* Your partner says that's the patriarchy talking. That only the worst kind of straight man would think that way. That she can see you differently in different contexts: with desire in moments of intimacy, with affection in moments of joy, with support in moments of pain or distress; and that none of those contexts affects the other. That if she does see your body that way, she'll only love and appreciate it more, for what it can do, the power of it, in making life and surviving.

You go into the hospital to be induced. You arrive early, like you've been told to, and lie alone in a room all day, waiting to see the doctor. You get breakfast. You get lunch. You get plenty of food, but no induction. Due to the pandemic, they're understaffed, and all the doctors are busy. By mid-afternoon you've read both the books you brought, pissed fifteen times, memorised the entirety of the room you're in, and your main worry is that the labour ward seems to be full and you will have to give birth in this room which you now hate with a powerful intensity. Your partner drives to the hospital after work and takes you to the canteen. You still haven't seen the doctor. You sit together, listening to the rain on the skylight, sharing chocolate eggs. *How's the baby?* your partner asks. *Still in there*, you say. *Must like it in there*, your partner says. *I'm amazed anyone ever comes out*, you say. *Never cold, never hungry, never tired. Nothing ever too loud or too bright, nothing ever—*

You're mid-sentence when you feel a gush between your legs, a gush which soaks through the thick maternity pad, through your thick maternity underwear, through your thick maternity tights. The nurse confirms it: your waters have broken. The baby has decided, all by itself. It's time to be born.

You go home. You get a takeaway burger from your favourite place: large, with fries, as a final treat. You put on a film and cuddle up to your partner. You're planning to get a good long sleep, to give yourself the energy for the labour, which you've been told won't start properly for hours. You're twenty minutes into the film and have only eaten half your burger when the first contraction hits.

The Birth

Your partner runs you a bath. When making the birth plan you said to her about the outdoor pool, the sea. She knows how you love to be in water.

You can't think of anything in the world you want less than to be in water. Fuck the bath, fuck the pool, fuck the sea. You rock on your hands and knees on the living-room rug, your voice a low moan, trying to catch your breath before the next contraction comes.

You feel it start to build and you say: *It's coming*. You say: *Oh no*. You say: *No no no no no*. And then you don't say anything because an agony like nothing you've ever felt before pulls through you.

You don't think the contractions feel like anything you've ever been told. They don't feel like bad period cramps. They don't feel like a tightening or a dull ache. They don't feel like bad shits. You planned to write a thoughtful description, a pretty description, about water, about the trips you took to the beach when you were pregnant, about all those hours you spent counting laps in the outdoor pool, about the waters inside your body and the baby floating like a selkie and how the contractions are like the lap and suck of the waves on the shore, and a contraction is coming again and it's not like that, it's not fucking like that at all, it's like fucking agony, that's all, it's not like anything, it's just pain.

Your partner times your contractions. They're four minutes apart, and so intense that when they reach their peak you can't speak or see, you can only hold on to yourself and to the floor like a ship's mast in a storm. She calls the maternity assessment line and they tell her that the contractions can't be that close together, it's too early. You know it's too fucking early. Tell your body.

They tell you not to come in yet, that the contractions will steady out soon, but you wait and breathe and groan and gasp through them, and your partner keeps timing them, and they get closer and closer together until she says, *Fuck this*, and she drives you to the hospital anyway.

There are no free beds so they put you in the triage room. It's very small and every time someone enters, your partner has to shuffle into the corner. There's a decal on the wall that says, in flowery cursive, with an actual literal silhouette of a flower petal: 'If you *believe* in yourself, anything is *possible*'. The contractions are two minutes apart now, and getting stronger. You're shaking uncontrollably. You're naked from the waist down. You think you must be crying because your face is wet. You can't sit or stand up or lie down, so you hunch over the black plasticky exam bed, your feet on a yellow sticker on the floor, bleeding right onto it. You ask for a sick bowl and you vomit so much that you overflow the bowl, vomit adding to your blood on the floor, and there's probably piss there too, you wouldn't be surprised, you can hear something plip-plipping out of you but you think it could just be more blood.

Your partner rubs your back, strokes your hair, breathes with you, goes and asks when there will be a bed for you, goes and asks if someone can come and check you, goes and asks for something to clear up your blood so you don't get it all over your feet. You come round from a contraction and your vision seeps back in. You look around for your partner but your eyes land on the decal on the wall. If you *believe* in yourself, anything is— You feel a contraction start to build again, and you hold on to the edge of the bed, hoping you won't fall into the smearing puddle of yourself.

You can't believe you told yourself you were good with pain. You've broken bones and you've ruptured a disc in your back and then walked around with it like that for six months and you've had surgery to remove that disc and you've had surgery to remove your tonsils and you've had surgery to remove several teeth from your overcrowded mouth and you thought you'd been in pain but you knew nothing, it was all nothing, nothing compared to this.

You don't understand how people can be in pain like this and not die.

You don't understand how people who have had babies have gone through this. Why aren't they dead? Why aren't they traumatised? Why aren't they still hunched over a plasticky bed unable to speak from the horror of it all?

You feel like you're going to die. You feel like that wouldn't be the worst thing. You want to run away from your body. You want to run out of this fucking room and away from that fucking decal.

You don't think you've ever hated anything (if you *believe* in yourself) as much as you hate that decal (anything is *possible*).

[As you write this you feel yourself pulling away, making it a story, the decal, the surreal ludicrousness of it, it's funny really, isn't it, what kind of fucking idiot put that stupid fucking decal there; but it didn't seem funny and it didn't seem surreal, it just seemed like you were going to die, you were terrified and in agony and going to die.]

Finally you're in a room. All you can do is lie on your side and wait for the next contraction. They tell you that the baby, who has been the correct way round for months, has turned back to back. The baby is pressing on your spine from the inside. They tell you that's why the pain feels so bad, and even in your haze of blood and pain and piss and sweat and shaking you think that makes sense, because it's not actually the contraction that's the problem, you could handle the contraction, although it's without a doubt the worst thing you've felt in your entire life; the problem is that as each contraction starts to fade out, at the point that you're meant to be catching your breath and calming ready for the next one, you feel this incredible, unbearable pushing feeling. It feels like a burning cannonball is trying to exit your body. You reach behind yourself, thinking you wouldn't be surprised to find your entire vagina, anus and lower back burst open.

You feel another contraction coming. You're afraid. There's a midwife and there's your partner but they're not doing anything, they're not helping you. The pain is coming again and no one is doing anything.

You say: *Please help me.*

You say: *It's pushing, it's pushing.*

You say: *I want to die,* and you know that's too far, your partner is frightened then, horrified even, but what you mean is that you need to be out of your body, you need to not be doing this, not feeling this, you want to crawl away from all this.

Your partner goes to the desk over and over and over, every ten minutes for the next few hours, to ask someone to come and help you. No one comes. Or if they do, you barely notice, in your pain and your panic, because they don't do the one thing you want them to do, which is make this stop. You suspect the midwives think you're making a fuss over nothing. They see this every day. All this pain, so bad you feel like you'll die – like you want to die – and you're just another person in labour. They've seen a dozen births already today, a dozen people who've wanted to die. Maybe one has. Or maybe that will be you.

[You find this hard to write, you find it hard to go back to that time, to that place, to those feelings in your mind and your body, but you have to live them again in order to write them; if there was a way to write them without having to live them again then you would, just like you would have leapt out of your body and run away if you could; but you can't, of course you can't.]

You remember your partner holding your hands. Telling you to breathe. You remember saying to her: *Please help me.* You remember telling her, as she reminds you to breathe deeply through the contractions, that the breathing doesn't work, it doesn't fucking work; you say it with a kind of wonder, a sense of betrayal that you'd been led to believe it would help, everyone said so, the midwife, your mum, and they all lied to you because you're doing it perfectly, just the way you practised for hours, and it doesn't fucking help at all.

You'd heard, aghast and gleeful, like when you hear a good ghost story, about the possibility of shitting during birth. You'd already decided that you weren't going to feel shame about that. That it was a natural process and nothing to be ashamed about. But now it's happening, now you've lost control of what feels like all your bodily processes, it doesn't even occur to you to consider shame. It's not that you feel yourself shit on the bed, feel someone – your partner or the midwife – clean it up and consciously, defiantly think, I refuse to be ashamed by this. It just doesn't occur to you. It doesn't matter. Nothing matters. You think you might die and your body isn't yours and nothing, none of this, is in anyone's control.

Your only concern is whether there is blood; you feel blood, always, leaking out of you, imagining it clotting and pooling beneath you even as your partner reassures you that isn't the case. You'd joked about swearing at her, blaming her: you did this to me, let's see you do this. But you can't. Even in your agony you can't. You ask her to help you even though you know she's already doing all she can to help you, which to you feels like absolutely fuck all; but what else can she do other than climb inside your body and feel all of this for you? Because she would be doing this if she could. She says: *I wish I could take the pain.* And if her body had let her, she'd be doing all of this, the pregnancy, the pain, the pushing. You can't blame her.

You feel another contraction coming.

You're afraid.

You say: *It's pushing, it's pushing.*

You say: *Please help me.*

You want to be assured that no, this is not right, it's not supposed to feel like this; but also it's all right, you'll be okay. But you can't get another dilation check for two hours. But you can't have gas and air because they can't properly sterilise the portable gas and air machine to make it Covid-safe. But you can only have two paracetamol.

[As you're writing this you stop; you get up out of your chair, you walk around the room, you get yourself a glass of water; you open the door and go outside and stand there for a moment, just breathing; you're making yourself go back there, to that series of rooms where you said you wanted to die and then you almost did die, or at least the baby inside you almost did; and anyway later you found out your friend who had a baby in a nearby hospital had portable gas and air so you don't know why they told you that, and you feel a lump in your throat when you remember how your voice sounded when you kept repeating, *Please help me, please help me, please.*]

Two paracetamol. Your contractions are two minutes apart and by the time they finally check you're seven centimetres dilated and you've had two fucking paracetamol.

You feel another contraction coming.

You're afraid.

You say: *It's pushing, it's pushing.*

You say: *Please help me.*

You've been in hospitals before. You've been in pain before. You've been prone, helpless, surrounded by doctors before. None of this scares you. This is the first time in your life you've been in a hospital and in pain and no one was trying to make the pain stop. No one, it seemed to you, was helping you.

When you were fifteen you tried to kill yourself. You took as many painkillers as you could find and went to bed. Your friend happened to call and you confessed to her. She told you to go and make yourself throw up while she called your parents, who were out. You fell asleep with your head in the toilet, having not managed to throw up (well, you certainly can throw up now). At the hospital you drank charcoal and retched while the doctor, unimpressed at this waste of his time, stood over you to make sure you kept it down. A mental health person of some kind asked you why you'd taken the pills; you said you just wanted to sleep. It wasn't true. You wanted to die. You wanted someone to help you so you wouldn't want to die any more. But you couldn't say that in front of your mum. You wanted this person to see through your lies and commit you somewhere. To forcibly help you. But you're not fifteen now and you know how to ask for help. So you ask and you ask and you ask. And no one helps you.

You've only been here for a few hours and the contractions are so close together. It's too fast. It's not right. Something is wrong, you think. Surely it's not meant to be like this. Why, you think, did no one tell me?

Before labour you noted this line in your phone: 'You can cope with anything if you know it will end'. It seemed smart to you, pithy. You thought you could use it when describing your labour.

It doesn't feel like it will end. It is everything. You understand now that you've never known pain before. You understand why people confess under torture. You would say or do anything to make the pain stop. But you can't make it stop. There is no escaping your body. There is no escaping this.

You feel another contraction coming.

You're afraid.

You say: *It's pushing, it's pushing.*

You say: *Please help me.*

As each contraction fades, your partner holds your hand, tries to get you to drink some water, strokes the hair back from your face. She tells you how proud she is of you, how she's in awe of you, how you're a warrior, a queen, a badass, the strongest person she's ever known. She tells you that you're doing an amazing job, but you know you're not, you'd rather not be doing this, you'd rather be doing anything else in the world other than this, and this doesn't even feel like something you're doing. It feels like something that's happening around you. A tidal wave, a tornado, an earthquake; some kind of natural disaster that you've unfortunately stumbled into.

[As you're writing this you feel yourself start to cry; you get up again and close your laptop and look out of the window for a moment; you feel like you have to remind yourself that it's over, you're not still in that series of little rooms stinking of your own blood and shit and terror; you're okay, you didn't die, the baby didn't die, you're okay.]

You can't believe that people eat food during labour. You can't believe they have conversations. You can't believe they listen to music or audiobooks. You can't believe they care, as the hypnobirthing lady suggested, about having scented oils or blankets with a certain texture. An entire brass band could be playing, plus a light show, and you wouldn't be aware of any of it. There is nothing except your body.

You don't feel angry. You don't shout or swear, though you thought you would. You just feel so unspeakably sad and alone. You just can't understand why no one is helping you.

It just has to be endured. There is nothing else to be done but—

You feel another contraction coming.

You're afraid.

You say: *It's pushing, it's pushing.*

You say: *Please help me.*

Finally the doctor comes. She asks what you would like, and you, shaking shitting pissing bleeding, unable to see when the pain reaches its peak, not screaming, not swearing, not being rude to anyone, not begging for an epidural, not demanding that someone get this fucking baby out of you, though you understand people in labour do some or all of these things and you fully understand why, you say: *I'd like to try some gas and air, if that's okay, please.*

You're wheeled backwards, bleeding and shaking, unable to raise your head, naked from the waist down, your lap covered with a small piece of paper, down a long hall past many

surprised strangers, into a labour room. In this room there
is a proper gas and air machine. You try it. It makes you feel
dizzy and sick. It doesn't take the pain away. Your partner
is still encouraging you to do the breathing from the hypnobirthing video, the breathing you spent hours practising
while bouncing on your yoga ball, while floating in the outdoor pool, and then you remember how you thought you'd
go there in your mind to stay calm, you remember how you
wanted a water birth, and how ridiculous all that seems
now, how all that planning and control was an illusion, and
everyone knew it was an illusion but no one told you.

The midwife puts a monitor in your vagina, attached to the
baby's head. The baby hasn't turned round the right way;
instead the baby has turned halfway, and is now stuck. The
baby's heart rate is dropping with each contraction. Your
body is trying to push the baby out, but the baby can't get
out. Your body is killing the baby.

You haven't been able to lie on your back but now they tell
you to, and you try but you can feel a contraction coming,
you can't bear it, you're sure this time you won't be able to
bear it, you try to roll onto your side but someone has put
your feet in stirrups so you can't. The contraction is coming
and you start crying. Someone, not your partner, you can't
see her, where is she, you can't see anything, where is she,
where is she, someone who isn't her holds the gas and air

mask over your face and tells you to breathe, breathe, breathe, and your head is spinning, and your whole self is somewhere up in the corner of the room, where is the baby, where is the baby—

[As you write this, months later, you still feel ashamed of how you behaved in labour, of your tears and your shit and your vomit, of how you pleaded for help, how you couldn't handle the pain, and no matter how much your partner tells you that the pain of the baby being back-to-back, the pain of the baby being stuck, was more than usual labour pain, you still don't believe her; didn't your mum birth you with only gas and air, you and your brother both; you should have been able to do it too; and you know, you've been told over and over, that no matter how much you pushed you were never going to get the baby out, you still think you failed by not doing it.]

It's bad now. You don't know how else to say that except it's bad. Your partner is pushed aside and your bed is wheeled out into the corridor and everyone speaks to you in calm voices and you're asking where the baby is and you can hear the heart monitor now, you can hear how slow the baby's heart is going.

[And you didn't know this at the time, you didn't know how bad it was, but later your partner tells you that she saw the doctor make a 'T' shape with her hands, meaning Theatre, meaning now, and that's how she knew it was bad.]

You're in theatre, everyone focused on their work around you, their work which is you, everyone speaking in low calm voices, hands moving fast, your body still shaking and shitting and puking and bleeding and pushing uncontrollably, your ears full of the too-slow throb of the baby's heart fading. Birth still isn't something that you're doing, and now it's not even something that's happening around you, now it's something that's being done to you. The doctor says you need an emergency section, there's no time to sign forms, do you consent. *Yes*, you say; *please*, you say, *get the baby out, please get the baby out.*

[You have to step away again, you have to take a moment to compose yourself, to tamp down your fear and your pain, even though you're not in pain now, there's nothing to be afraid of now, you know you made it and you know the baby made it and everyone is fine, everything is fine.]

The baby's heart rate is so slow and the plastic taste of the plastic gas and air mask fills your mouth and the doctor puts a needle into your neck.

The next thing, the very next second, without sleep, without dreams, you're waking and a voice is saying: *Here's the baby!*

For a second you think: What baby?

[You've seen photos your partner took of this moment: you, face red, eyeliner smeared, glasses sitting wonky because you still have the oxygen tubes in your nose, other mystery tubes emerging from your clothes; she took the photo to remember this moment, the first time you properly met the baby; but all you can focus on is your eyes, the way they're utterly fucked, out in space somewhere, unfocused, but still looking at the baby; you don't remember this but your partner tells you that when they said to you, *Here's the baby*, you looked up at the corner of the room, as if you expected the baby to be up there, floating.]

But there is a baby. It's your baby. It's very small. You hold it. You touch its face. You touch its hands. You cry, and you think it's tears of happiness, but you're not sure, you're not sure of anything at all.

[You find out later that your partner wasn't allowed in the room during the emergency C-section; that she had to wait down the corridor, 3 a.m. and all alone, not knowing if you were dead, not knowing if the baby was dead, and all she could do was pace circles and call your mum and her mum and her dad and her sister, and she didn't even have any information to give them; and when the baby was out she still wasn't allowed in the room, it turns out they got the baby out fast but then it took a full hour to stitch you up after; but a nurse took pity on her and came to find her to say that you were okay and let her creep down the corridor and listen at the door to the baby crying, the baby out and crying, the baby alive and you alive, and she was crying then too.]

You and your partner and the baby are in a recovery room. You must have been wheeled in there at some point, but you don't remember. A midwife comes in. She asks if you want to breastfeed and you say, *Yes*. Before the birth you didn't think breastfeeding was important either way but now you're positive you absolutely must breastfeed. The midwife lifts up your bare breast and pushes your nipple into the baby's mouth. The baby resists, tries to pull back. The midwife pushes harder. You don't think this seems right but what do you know, you've never fed anyone with your body before. Perhaps babies need convincing. Perhaps they need to be forced not to let themselves starve to death. Your nipple slips again out of the baby's mouth. The midwife sighs and looks at her watch. She says: *You can't do it. I'll have to give the baby formula. But any more and baby won't want the breast.* You watch as she feeds the baby a tiny amount of formula milk with a syringe. You, the complainer, the sayer, the one who always speaks up, who always demands that people respect her, who always at least tries to get what she wants, who has already come up with sassy responses for anyone who asks about how two women got pregnant, anyone who uses the term 'natural childbirth', anyone who tries to judge or shame you in any way – you say nothing. Your partner, who routinely calls out strangers for pushing in queues, for not saying excuse me, for pissing in the alley behind your flat on football match days – she says nothing. None of this seems right to you, but you don't know what's right. You don't know how it's meant to go and how it's not meant to go. You don't know anything. The midwife hasn't even left the room before you start crying.

It's 6 a.m., you've been conscious for less than an hour, and your partner has to leave. You're going to the ward and because of Covid restrictions she can only come at visiting hours, which begin at 10 a.m. For the next four hours, you're on your own with an hour-old baby. Your partner has been awake all night, and you know that if you don't specifically tell her to go home and rest, she'll wait in the car outside until visiting hours. You tell her to go; sleep, eat, tell everyone that you and the baby are still alive. She kisses you both, and she's gone, and you're wheeled from one room of strangers into another room of strangers.

The baby is asleep, so you sleep.

You didn't see the birth. Your partner didn't see the birth. You haven't met anyone who saw the birth. Who was the first person to see the baby's face? Who was the first person to hear the baby's voice? You have no idea.

You want to make it all mean something. The birth, the labour, the miraculous emergence of new life. But you weren't awake. You weren't even asleep and dreaming. You were not there at all.

The Baby

1

You're so tired you think of nothing. A sweet floating emptiness. A drowsy completeness. You doze. You sip water from a plastic cup. You hold the baby on your chest. You stay like that for hours. Time stretches and unstructures. You don't have to get up to pee because you still have a catheter in. You try to put food in your mouth but don't want it. Your tongue is still numb but that's not why. It's the floating. The nothing.

The blue curtains stay pulled around your bed and you drift, you and the baby together on this ocean. You're not meant to fall asleep holding the baby but you do; you feel like you're never properly asleep anyway, never properly awake, just drifting, always. The nurses come in every few hours to check your blood pressure and give you pills. You don't really know anything about babies but you know that they cry if they want things. The baby doesn't cry. The baby blinks and snuffles and mewls. You bring the baby to your nipple a dozen times an hour. The baby isn't interested. There's no latching. There's no milk. You don't have any nappies and the baby isn't crying for a nappy change and if the baby isn't eating anything then what would even be in a nappy? No one seems concerned about nappies. No one seems concerned about milk. Women come behind the blue curtains – midwives, you assume, or nurses, though you don't actually know – and show you how to hold your breast, show you how to hold the baby, show you how to guide the nipple in, explain how it should feel. It doesn't feel like that. You feel a pulling, a tug somewhere in the unsettled depths of yourself, the inner parts that strangers have now seen but you have not. You can't tell if the baby has managed to get any milk or not. You squeeze your nipple hard, hard, hard until it hurts, until a tiny drop of golden liquid begins to form, looking exactly like the condensed milk you put in your coffee when you went to that book festival in Malaysia and met that ridiculously beautiful Chinese man with the same birthday as you. You wonder what he's doing now. You wonder if he has a child; you never asked. You catch the drop on your pinkie finger and put it into the baby's mouth, so you can know the baby at least got something from you.

You were prepared to not instantly bond with baby. You'd been warned. With your amber-warning mental health history, your traumatic birth, your unconsciousness when the baby was pulled from your body – it's not unusual, even likely.

When you write a book, people who haven't written books ask you: *How did you feel when you first held your book?* And you smile and talk about your pride, your satisfaction, your sense of a long journey coming to an end or a dream finally realised. But the truth is you didn't really feel any of those things when you held a book you'd written. Not the first book and not any of the ones after that. The first moment of holding a book you write is curiously hollow. You'd thought it might be the same for holding a baby you made. You wondered if you'd hold the baby, the way you've held books, and think: Is that it? I thought I'd feel more.

But it's not the same at all. You adore the baby. Instantly, completely. On the long twilit nights in the maternity ward you hold the baby close to you and drip your tears onto the tiny face. When you hold the baby, you feel everything, you feel love spill out of you, so much love you feel like you could choke on it, holding the baby tight and thinking, I love you I love you I love you I love you.

You are newborn. The whole world is strange and wonderful to you. You watch the baby explore the world with those new eyes, new mouth, new hands. The baby wants to know the world, but you only want to know the baby.

Your partner comes to visit. She arrives before visiting hours start and leaves long after they end, hiding behind the blue curtain with you and the baby, staying quiet in the hope no one will notice any of you.

You watch her with the baby. You are exhausted and blissful and indignant and ecstatic and accomplished and confused and aching and altered and still, incredibly, you haven't burst into flame. You watch as she holds the baby close. You watch as she changes the baby's nappy. *Sleep*, she says, and you do. You lie back on your clammy hospital bed, the blue light soft around you, and you listen as she sings to the baby the songs she used to sing to your bump. You fall asleep almost instantly, knowing that you've handed the baby off to someone else to watch over. The baby is real. The baby is okay.

She leaves, and you have to wake up. There's no one else to look after the baby except you. You realise that it's been twelve hours since you got to the ward; that you are naked, sweating, bleeding; that you've barely eaten, that you've only had a cup of tea because one of the other women on the ward brought you one; that you haven't brushed your teeth or washed your face; that you still have the remnants of eyeliner on from before the birth, and you remember putting that eyeliner on, how you'd do your make-up in the mornings after rubbing cream on your belly, and the bump would press against the full-length mirror and leave a little oily belly print. You wonder if your partner has cleaned it off, or if it will still be there when you and the baby go home.

You don't know what to call the place where the baby came out. You hesitantly call it your wound, but this seems overly dramatic. You try calling it your scar, but it's not a scar yet. Your cut, but that seems oddly sexual, and the misogyny and violence of that doesn't escape you. When you breastfeed you feel the stutter and pang of your uterus shrinking. Being pregnant, every day you were growing. For almost ten months, you swelled and bloomed. Now what are you doing? Are you diminishing? Your body feels tight, secretive. You think about how you've now been cut open, at almost the same latitude, at the back and the front of your body. *No weightlifting for me*, you joke to the midwife, though really what you want to do is not joke at all, but have someone tell you with some certainty if and when you can expect to regain feeling across the entire centre of your body. It doesn't hurt, though perhaps it will when the painkillers wear off. Right now, it's just numb. The midwife casually tells you she's still numb from her own C-section twenty years ago. You don't know if that's meant to make you feel better, or feel bad for asking.

You finally get out of bed a full day after the birth. It's the first time you've stood up since becoming not-pregnant. You feel the drool of blood down your legs and onto your feet. You've bled through two maternity pads, each as thick as a steak. You waddle to the shared bathroom as fast as you can, but you still leave a trail of bloody footprints. You start cleaning yourself up, and of course that's when the baby wakes up, and you grab as much toilet paper as you can and shuffle fast across the ward floor, trying to wipe up your vaginal blood, trying to get to the baby fast, and you stand up and lift the baby out of the cot, and you feel more blood flowing out of you and through the new pad, and there's blood all down your legs, and you're standing in blood, and there's blood on your hands and you try to hold the baby close, to stroke that tiny face without getting your blood on it. And the most amazing thing to you is that none of it hurts.

Less than forty-eight hours after arriving at hospital, you're discharged. You haven't changed a nappy, success-fully breastfed or eaten a meal. The physiotherapist comes by and tells you not to use your core muscles to sit up, which is exactly what you've been doing every time you need to get out of bed to tend to the baby. *Oh*, says the physiotherapist. *Well, try not to do it from now on.* You imagine your muscles, torn and fraying, ripped open every time you move.

Your partner brings the going-home outfit you both chose for the baby. A little striped hat and booties, leggings, a buttercup-yellow jumper. It all looked impossibly tiny when you picked it out. How strange it feels to see the clothes on an actual, real baby, not just a figment of your imagination.

Your partner charms the nurses, just as she charms everyone. You're relieved, as you hope it will make them like you more, that the golden shine of her likeability might make you gleam, just a little bit, in reflection. You're aware the maternity ward is understaffed and you are taking up a much-needed bed; that you are puffy and exhausted, not charming, not funny, not maternal. You're thinking about that amber warning. You smile at everyone, trying to be good good good, trying to be nice nice nice, and the baby looks so wholesome in the little outfit, and your partner looks so capable holding the car seat. You're a good family, a nice family.

Your partner drives you all home. You sit in the back seat, one arm stretched out to the baby, one arm pressed across your numb and empty centre. When you get home, your belly print is still on the mirror, smeared now, ghostly.

2

In hospital, you didn't believe anyone who told you that you handled labour well. That the baby was beautiful. That the baby was thriving. That you were doing anything right. Now, at home, you see other people holding the baby. Your mum, your stepdad, your partner's mum, your partner's stepdad, your partner's dad, your partner's stepmum, your great-aunt, your partner's aunt, your donor, your donor's partner, your this, your that, your everyone. It takes a village to raise a baby, and here is yours. One by one they come by to hold the baby. *I love you*, they all say to the tiny upturned face.

Finally you see the baby properly. The baby is beautiful. A truly beautiful baby. The rosebud mouth and tiny fat nose.

The huge dark eyes, no difference between pupil and iris. You'd thought they'd be bright blue, like your eyes and your dad's eyes and your grandad's eyes. But they're not that, and they're not the colour of your donor's eyes either. They're entirely the baby's own.

When the baby is three days old, you all go out for brunch. This seems to you, writing this later, an act of madness. You had major surgery three days ago. A human being exited your body three days ago. But at the time it feels like a perfectly logical decision. Not even a decision, really: you and your partner are hungry, you like going out for brunch, you like this brunch place – you often joke the baby is made entirely of egg and kale rolls, you ate so many of them during the pregnancy. Going out for brunch is just a thing that you do, so you do it. The baby sleeps, tiny and content, in a carrier on your partner's chest. Everyone coos and fusses. Your partner glows. You feel tired and sore and proud.

You smell of milk all the time. Sweet, like a fancy cake shop. You hug a friend who's come to visit the baby and you smell milk rising from you like perfume.

You wrote a lot about pregnancy before you were pregnant. Often the characters were pregnant by something not-human. A bear. A wolf. A sea creature. You didn't know at the time why you did this, but now it makes sense to you. Now that you've been through pregnancy, you find the supernatural speaks more truth than realism does. You can say: the baby is this number of weeks old, is this size, has this amount of hair, is doing these things. It's all true, it's all real. But look at the baby. Just look. Holding a little knitted ball in those tiny hands. Staring out at the world with those deep-sea eyes. How can the lucid, everyday world explain this? The wonder, the curiosity, the recognition. The baby has lived inside your body, and you've only just met. The baby is your familiar, and deeply unfamiliar.

When you were heavily pregnant and heavily frustrated with your lack of writing progress, you pitched four new novel ideas to your editor. She has three children, so you asked her whether it was better to think about these ideas now, or wait until the baby was older. You were optimistic, but also you'd seen many friends' writing careers pause for several years after babies, and assumed you'd be the same. Your editor said to expect many nights spent walking in circles with a sleepless baby, during which it's nice to have something to think about, and it might as well be a book idea. Here you are, a sleepless baby, circling the floor, and you think of nothing. Smooth brain. Lovely empty mind. The idea of developing a novel is laughable; you can barely make a sentence.

But you're not as upset about not-thinking as you thought you'd be. Not as upset as you should be, maybe. You find it quite nice to not think. You used to secretly feel scorn for women who were satisfied by mothering. Who were made complete by nappies and milk, dinners and dishes, scrubbing dirt and dust and other people's shit off things. (Feminism, after all, doesn't mean that you magically only ever think nice things about other women.) Then, as a backlash, also secretly, you felt scorn for the people who scorned those people. What did they know, anyway? What could they tell from the outside looking in? Now you're on the other side of the glass, and you find that you like it. Not the shit specifically, though the shit is not as big a deal as you expected. You like changing the baby's little nappy and choosing the baby's little outfit and pushing the baby's massive pram in the park. Are you stupid? Are you just a womb with legs? Is this all hormones? Are you just tired? It's nice to just be. To be present. To know what you're meant to do in this moment.

Or maybe you're not upset because you're so sure you can get it back. Eventually, your mind will return, your dreams and ideas and thoughts that follow on from one another like train carriages, uninterrupted. You're sure it's all waiting for you, tucked away at the back of the cupboard. Like your body, which you were sure you could return to unscathed, though it's now abundantly clear to you that you'll never have that body again.

The baby still won't latch on. You've decided that breast-feeding is the most important thing in the world. Your partner takes over all the domestic chores: cleaning, cooking, changing nappies, walking the dog. You finally agreed to let the baby have some formula milk, and your partner does all that too: the boiling, the mixing, the sterilising. You have two jobs: heal, and pump milk. You're not that bothered about the healing; all you care about is watching the milk drip into the pump bottle, desperate for the line of milk to reach higher. You sit on the breast pump for as long as you can bear. In the evenings you and your partner watch foreign TV shows together; that way you can tell yourselves you have the subtitles on for translation, not just because you can't hear the dialogue over the sound of the pump. Like an irritating song, the pump's rhythm catches in your mind. To distract you, your partner does dances and sings songs to the rhythm of the pump. You laugh and allow yourself to be distracted. You join in the songs and shimmy your shoulders to the pump's rhythm, both your hands holding the pump's plastic cup tight to your breast. The moment your partner leaves the room, you look at where the line of milk has reached, despairing that you can't get it any higher.

The dog is so gentle. She sniffs around the baby, careful not to get too close. She looks up at you with her soft brown eyes, checking: Is this okay? You're not sure if she knows what the baby is, but she knows to be gentle.

The baby still won't latch on. You speak to the midwife, and then another midwife, then a health visitor, then another health visitor. They all show you different holds, different techniques; they tell you various pieces of advice, most of which contradict each other. Your breasts know what to do. When you're on the pump they're reluctant, grumbling; but as soon as the baby's skin touches yours, your nipples start leaking. You hold the baby the way you've been shown – all the ways, one after another, the world's least elegant dance routine. The milk beads and dribbles fast from your nipple, smearing on your hands, making them sticky and sweet-smelling. But there's still no proper latching, no suck. Your body is trying its best. The milk drips on the baby's pursed-up face and protesting fists; on your lap, on your couch; through your bra, through your clothes. Your body made this for the baby, and it's all being wasted. The baby is hungry, and cries, and you cry too.

You attach yourself to the breast pump and listen to its hateful song. You watch your partner feed the baby with a bottle of your milk. The baby's hands open and close; the baby's eyelids flutter in ecstasy. You tell yourself that's you,

you're feeding the baby. But you're over here, and they are over there.

You are wildly in love with the baby. All you want to do is see the baby, smell the baby, touch the baby. You thought you knew love. But not like this.

You ask your partner: *Do you think the baby likes me?*

She replies: *The baby loves you. The baby doesn't know anything other than you.*

You spend so long looking at the baby's face that when, at the end of the day, you look at yourself in the bathroom mirror, you're surprised to see your own face and not the baby's.

You haven't read much that covers the early, dreamy, insane days with a newborn. It makes sense, because what time is there to write? To think? To notice? Then soon it's over, and amnesia sets in. So you try to notice. You try to think. But your thoughts are treacly, slow and sweet.

You didn't enjoy baths during pregnancy, as you could only have the water at body temperature, and that felt at best unsatisfying and at worst faintly disgusting. But now you can have the bath as hot as you like. You lie in the water, your skin bright red and swollen, and let your head swim. You watch as thin streams of milk and blood leak from your body, ribboning in the water. Is the water cleaning you, or are you dirtying the water?

Later, writing this book, you find in your notes that description of lying in the bath and watching the milk ribbon out of you. You don't remember it happening, but there it is in your notes. You don't think that you not remembering it means it didn't happen. You wouldn't have written it if it hadn't happened. There are plenty of parts of your life like that: ghost times, barely remembered, their existence unprovable. But still. Should you be writing it in this book if you don't remember it? You delete the section. Then you restore it. Delete. Restore. You've imagined it so thoroughly now that you're even more confused about whether it really happened.

You picture throwing the baby. Not just dropping, but throwing. At the fireplace, at the wardrobe door, onto the sharp corner of the coffee table. You look into the baby's huge trusting eyes and imagine a needle going into them, just at the inner corners. You had problems with intrusive thoughts when you were younger, to do with scissors and the webbing between your fingers, to do with razor blades and the backs of your calves. You thought they'd gone away, but maybe nothing ever really goes away.

You keep thinking about scurvy. You think about something you read once, that when you get scurvy all your old wounds open. You've had three surgeries: your tonsils out, a ruptured disc in your back, a C-section; these new scars add to the old self-harm ones down your arms. If you got scurvy, you think, you'd die fast. Your throat full of blood, your guts falling out, your hands slippery and smeared red. But your partner has never had an operation, has never broken a bone, is as scar-free as it's reasonable for an adult to be. You remind yourself that it will be okay, because she'd be okay. If you bled out, she could look after the baby.

You tell your partner. Not about the needle, not the throwing, but just that you're imagining bad things happening to the baby. She says that every time she carries the baby down the stairs, she has vivid images of a sudden drop, a thudding onto the century-old stone steps, her body falling onto the baby and crushing every bone in that tiny body.

But you won't, you say. *Neither will you*, she replies.

3

The midwife says your blood pressure is high, and sends you back to the maternity assessment centre. You wait in the triage room. This hateful room is haunting you. Or you are haunting it.

It's still small, but it seems bigger now that you're alone. No baby. No partner. Just you and your body. You remember standing on that yellow sticker, puke and blood and shit coming out of you, the shaking, the crying, the helplessness. 'If you *believe* in yourself, anything is *possible*.' You don't know if you've ever hated anything more than that decal. You allow the rage, the terror, the trauma to fill you. To flow through you. To overflow.

Then you take a photo of the decal and send it to your group chat. You've already told them about standing on the yellow sticker, bleeding on your feet, overflowing the puke bowl. The group chat fills with emoji responses as they join you in mocking the decal. They reply: *live laugh bleed uncontrollably*. They reply: ✨ live ✨ love ✨ vom

You tell them about bleeding through the steak-thick maternity pads and your trail of bloody footprints across the maternity-ward floor. You tell them about being wheeled backwards down the hospital corridor, naked from the waist down, vagina gushing blood, your lap covered with a small piece of paper. The story you're telling of the birth is taking on Gothic-horror tones, and you like it. You like that it's a story. You like that it's Gothic and gory. You like that it's surreal and funny. You like, most of all, that you're alive and so is the baby.

But you're making it a story. And it wasn't a story. It wasn't Gothic and it wasn't funny. Trauma is an eternal present tense and even now you feel the echoes of labour pains in your body. You fear the pain coming back. You fear not being helped. You thought you were going to die. You wanted to die.

But isn't it nicer to make it a story? Aren't ghost stories fun?

The nurse comes in. She has a leopard-print faux-fur pen, which you find awful but say is lovely, just to have something to discuss as she velcroes on the blood pressure cuff. She puts you in a bed on a ward and says the doctor will be there soon, which means sometime between now and, probably, midnight. Everyone around you is heavily pregnant and hooked up to a foetal heartbeat monitor. Most of them are talking in low tones to their husbands or boyfriends. The nurse pulls the curtains shut. Waiting in bed, reading a book about pregnancy which you realise you have at some point, appropriately enough, spilled breast milk on, surrounded by the staticky murky sounds of unborn babies' hearts, you hear the woman in the next bed start to slur. All you can see is the lilac paper curtains around you. Her partner calls out, his panic barely evident, *Excuse me? Can you please come here?* The midwives bustle around her, voices soft like they're speaking to a child, *Sweetheart, my love, do you know where you are? Let's just get this little cuff on.* You imagine – or are you imagining? – that the sound of her baby's heart is slowing.

You don't know what the nurses did, but the woman is coming out of it, her voice steady now. She apologises, over and over, *I'm sorry, I'm so sorry, I think I need to go to the toilet.* You think of yourself, two rooms down from here, shaking shitting pissing bleeding, sure you were going to die, wanting to die, saying, *I'd like to try some gas and air, if that's okay, please.* On TV, people scream and swear when they're in pain or afraid. In real life – or in this maternity ward, anyway – people hide their terror. They say please. They say sorry. If everyone is still minding their manners, it can't be that bad, can it?

Finally the doctor comes. Your blood pressure is fine. You're sent home. *It was just nice to get some quiet reading time*, you say to the doctor. And it's true: you have enjoyed having several hours, just you and a book. But then your partner comes to pick you up, and she brings the baby, who is far too young to recognise you or respond to you, but who you are sure is happy to see you, who maybe even smiles to see your face, and it's the best bit of the day.

When you see other people pushing newborn babies in prams, or toting them around in carriers, you feel a moment of awe. A silence falls between you. The hush of things that can't be spoken. When people say, *No one is talking about this*, maybe what they mean is, *Please don't make me talk about this*. You know now what trauma they've been through. You know about their scars. You wonder that they're still alive. You find it incredible now that pregnancy, birth and parenthood are seen as natural, cosy – twee even. Cutesy. Safe and a little dull. But now you know what birth is. It's the inside of your body on the outside. It's the most violent body experience other than death. It's looking at death and not blinking.

Everyone who's ever given birth has done that. Made something from nothing. Seen death, and made life instead. No wonder that, throughout history, and still now, some men try to control it, deny it, force it. No wonder they fear it. You've done it, and you fear it.

But it's all better now! we chirp, in our floaty maternity dresses with the clip-down top for breastfeeding, our bodies bleeding from somewhere hidden. *It was hard but it was worth it!* we grin, expertly unfolding a buggy with one hand, our babies gurning and drooling, our scars hidden. *We're okay now! At least the baby is okay! Everything is okay!*

You think about googling C-section surgery. Maybe there's a video, or photos, or at least a detailed description of the process. You want to write a bit about it; the image of you, cut open on a table, your baby tugged from you, body and placenta and umbilical all in one, held aloft, finally breathing; strangers holding your uterus in their hands, piling your slippery purple intestines back into the cavity of you, stitching you gently back up. How again, for the third time in your life, strangers have cut you open and taken things out of you; strangers have seen parts of you that you will never see yourself. But you don't. You find, to your surprise, that you can't. You remind yourself there's a reason they put a screen up during a C-section.

But still. You want connection. You want a mirror. You tentatively google 'emergency C-section' and find plenty of people talking about their emergency C-sections, and you dive into the pool in relief. But then you emerge, coughing, enraged. These are not emergency C-sections. These are unplanned C-sections. These happen with epidurals, and partners present, and the birth mother awake and getting to see the baby right when it's born. No one is panicking or crying. They get tea and toast after. What is this shit? This isn't what you want. You want to comment, *That isn't a fucking emergency C-section.* You want to comment, *Please be accurate in your description of emergency C-sections.* (You're aware that you're gatekeeping emergency C-sections, but you don't care.) You want to press your hands into someone else's blood and then look at it. You want to hear about someone else almost dying, thinking they were dying, wanting to die, but surviving. You want to compare their scars to your own. You don't know if you want to look at theirs and think, I'm glad mine aren't that bad, or if you want to think, How wonderful; mine are much, much worse.

You remember, in labour, saying to your partner: *I can't do it, I can't do it.* And you really believed that you couldn't.

You still believe you can't. You think of your dad's death; how a few years before he died, when he was suicidal and threatening to go out into the woods in winter and take off his clothes and freeze to death, you wrote in your journal, 'If he dies, I will die. My heart will simply stop beating.' And then he did die, and you didn't. You knew you couldn't go on without him, and then you did.

Your wedding anniversary is the same date as your dad's birthday. Every year when it comes around you feel a mix of emotions that, every year, you choose not to linger on or examine. The baby's birthday is the anniversary of the day you both almost died.

You keep coming back to your dad's death. It was ten years ago and you're over it, you really thought you were over it, even though out loud you tell grieving friends that, of course you never get over it, grief never really ends. But for you, you thought, it actually had ended. That period of time between knowing things were not okay and your family all agreeing to switch off the life support. That period of time between the first contraction and being handed a baby. That endless, compressed time in a hospital room that changed you instantly, utterly.

You arrange a video-chat session with your therapist. You like her; you chose her pretty much at random from a website of therapists, but it's turned out that she's the perfect therapist for you. She's a mother of three, but isn't preachy about 'natural' childbirth or breastfeeding. She's firm against your anxiety and gentle about your intrusive thoughts. She's become an important addition to your baby-raising village. You tell her about the birth. The blood, the pain, the fear, the unbelievable, unbearable, overwhelming love.

Your therapist says it's good that you don't blame baby for the birth trauma. You're struck by this, as it didn't even occur to you to blame the baby. You don't connect the birth and the baby. It wasn't the baby's first experience; it was only yours. Your therapist says it's a sort of grief. That you have to allow yourself to acknowledge this image you had of the perfect birth, and to feel sad about the fact that you can never have it. You didn't realise, when you chose her, that she specialised in this. What is this, exactly? Can anyone ever specialise in what happens to you, except you?

You tell more people about the birth: your friend who's had three babies of her own, your friend who's had no babies and never will, your cousin, your upstairs neighbour, the midwife, the other midwife, the other other midwife, your partner, over and over, even though she was there and already knows. Each time you tell it, it becomes blunter, rounded and softened from use. It becomes almost funny – not the part where the baby almost died, but the part where you pooped everywhere, the part with the wall decal. It is kind of funny, now you think about it.

We're okay now. At least the baby is okay. Everything is okay. The more you tell it, the more it's just a story. The way you tell it, compulsively, to anyone who asks, whether or not they really want to hear it, again and again and again. You don't know what you want to find in this retelling. You don't know whether you want the story to change, or just for its edges to soften. For the tide of your telling to wash over it, making it wave-worn, blunting it like sea-glass.

4

You can't see your wound as your belly hasn't deflated yet, but you're glad of that. The whole area feels like a disaster. It's covered by a large white sticking plaster, the size of a loaf of bread. You know that eventually you'll have to peel it off and see the horror underneath, but you don't want to. You don't even like other people looking at it. You won't let your partner see it. After much convincing, you let your mother-in-law, a retired nurse, see it for a brief second. She says it seems to be healing, but it doesn't feel that way to you. You worry about your wound unzipping, your intestines flopping wetly out. You worry about an instrument left inside you, your womb slowly shrinking around it until its contours are visible through your skin. You feel the echoes of labour pains in your body.

The health visitor lifts your belly to look at your wound, and suddenly it splits. You can't see or feel this, but she tells you. You imagine the mouth of it opening, your insides coming out. You imagine it gaping and drooling, blood and pus, your body a Gothic horror once more. You don't need more stitches, she says; you just need to rest so it can heal. This seems ridiculous to you. They told you the same thing in the hospital, but how were you supposed to rest when you had a newborn baby to look after? When your partner was only allowed to visit for a few hours a day? When you had to get up, over and over, to lift the baby from the cot? After your back operation, you were on bed rest for a month. After your C-section, you rested for a few hours.

You feel exhausted, headachy, irritable. Could you have an iron deficiency? Could you have an infection in your wound? You get blood tests. It's hard to know what's normal and what's sickness. Nothing is normal any more, but it's the most normal thing in the world. You're just so tired. Your head just aches so much. But the tests come back, and you don't have an iron deficiency, and you don't have an infection. You just have a baby.

You realise that no one is really looking after you, including you. Your wound has opened because you're moving around too much. You miss several doses of your medications, because you and your partner both lose track of time. You forget to eat, drink, shower, dress, pee, breathe. You have so much help – your partner does all the housework and most of the baby care; people from both sides of your family visit daily; friends bring groceries and adorable gifts. Everyone – including you – thinks they're helping, because they're all making sure the baby is okay. And if the baby is okay, that means you're okay too.

Here's what you want. You know it's selfish and you can't have it and you can't even ask for it. You want to take to your bed. Ideally you want the white room, the white sheets, the white curtains wafting in the breeze, the soft-footstepped nurses with lots of pills. But you'd settle for your own bedroom, with its deep-blue walls, its milk-sticky sheets, the dog dozing on the floor. You just want to be able to stay in it. But you can't. You can't. Everyone says you can – that they will help to make sure that the baby is fed and clean, that the dishes are washed, that your partner eats and sleeps. Everyone says you can just rest. But that's ridiculous. How can you lie in bed when your baby needs you? How can you sleep when the baby is not asleep? You can't. It's that simple: no matter what anyone says, you can't.

You cry many times a day, and sometimes it's a scene from a comedy, and sometimes a tragedy.

You cry when you put music on for the baby to listen to during a feed and a sentimental love song comes on and you drip tears right on the baby's face because it's true, finally you understand the meaning of the words, and you repeat them to the baby between sobs, songs about always loving. About never leaving. About baby, my baby, love you baby, always my baby. You cry because you're a shit mother and you don't deserve the baby, you don't deserve anything, you purposely sit in positions that hurt and when your C-section wound throbs with pain you force yourself to stay still.

You cry when you have a bath two days after you stop expressing and you feel the milk drip from your breasts and go into the bath water, wasted, this precious thing your body made for your baby that you're wasting because you're selfish, you can't handle pain and you don't care about your baby.

You cry because you love the baby so much, your heart is beating outside your body now, you can't bear it, how can anyone be expected to bear it?

While you were pregnant, someone you know had an abortion. The embryo was about the same size as yours. It was the right choice for her, as your choice was right for you. Having a child has made you more pro-choice, even as your belief in being pro-choice was so strong you didn't think it could increase. But it has. You loved being pregnant, despite the discomfort, despite your anxiety. But it was also the hardest thing you've ever done. The baby was very much planned and wanted and provided for; your partner was just as excited and ready as you were; your family and friends were all willing to be your village. And it was still the hardest thing you've ever done. No one should have to do that if they don't want to.

You've stopped trying to breastfeed. The baby just couldn't latch on, no matter what you tried, and wasn't gaining enough weight. Wasn't thriving. You want, more than anything in the world, for the baby to thrive. So you switch to formula. It's not that your partner is pleased about you not breastfeeding, exactly. But you don't think she's un-pleased either. *I want you to do whatever is best for you, and for the baby*, she says. You think you would have tried to breastfeed until the end of time, if it weren't for the baby being at risk. Now that your milk has dried up, you see that you were obsessed; that breastfeeding was never that important to you, but it became another stick to beat yourself with.

Do you want to feed the baby? you ask your mum, your stepdad, your partner's mum, your partner's stepdad, your partner's dad, your partner's stepmum, your great-aunt, your partner's aunt, your donor, your donor's partner, your this, your that, your everyone. *Yes!* they all say, and they do. You love to see them nurture the baby like this. You made the baby in your body; you fed and grew the baby's body for ten months. But now it's not all on you.

You do miss your bump, though. You miss being a precious thing. You miss the momentum of your body moving through the supermarket aisles like a galleon. You miss always being productive even when you're asleep. You miss the baby being all yours.

Your partner does most of the night feeds so that you can rest. You know that if she could, she'd breastfeed. She wants to be exhausted, sleepless, inconvenienced. She wants swollen ankles and aching nipples. She wants to be undeniably, physically a part of this baby. She's been denied the pregnancy; she at least wants that.

Who do you want to be? you ask your partner as she rocks the baby to sleep. *Mama*, she says. *Is that okay? Can I be Mama?* So you're Mum, and your partner is Mama. We don't have a word for the non-birth mother. That's the thing about being queer parents, the good and the bad thing: there are no words, so you get to choose the ones you want.

But motherhood is about so much more than growing a baby in your body. Parenthood, too; but motherhood specifically. The baby knows Mama and Mum equally; has cried for you specifically, and for your partner specifically. You find yourself less and less attached to the concept of biology. Your partner is there every evening when the baby falls asleep and every morning when the baby wakes up. For the first few months of life, she held the baby's hand through every night. She plays with the baby, sings to the baby, soothes the baby, entertains the baby, teaches the baby. She is a mother, just as you are.

A woman is not the ability to bear a child, or the ability to want to. It seems ludicrous to you to have to state that, like saying 'a circle is round' or 'red is a colour', but it seems to you that every day there is some person trying to reduce women to biology. You are not more of a woman because you could make a child in your body. Your partner is not less of a woman because she couldn't.

And even though you produced a child with your body, even though you are most people's exact definition of a mother, you still struggle to use the word, just like you struggled to say you were pregnant. You once asked a family member how she felt about her recent retirement, thinking she'd talk about taking up new hobbies, sleeping in, feeling free, feeling wonderful; but she said: *I feel a bit lost, actually. I went from being someone's daughter, to someone's sister, to someone's mother, to someone's employee. And now I have to figure out who I am on my own terms.*

You were fascinated, as you'd never felt anything like that. You'd never thought to define yourself through other people. If you were asked, you'd say: *I'm a writer, and I have a baby.* You wouldn't think to call yourself the baby's mum.

You're irritated by articles and advice that mention husbands, boyfriends or partners 'supporting' the birth mother, as if it's primarily her responsibility, and the baby's other parent is just helping. You get an image of the birth mother holding up a stone baby, incredibly heavy, knee-snappingly heavy, muscle-shakingly heavy; and the other parent comes along and props wooden laundry poles under her armpits. There you go. Helping.

Your partner takes the late-night feeds; you take the early-morning ones. At dusk she says to you: *Would you like a glass of wine or would you like to sleep?* At dawn you say to her: *Would you like a cup of tea or would you like to sleep?*

You love the early mornings. The baby falls back to sleep after the first feed. You lie there: your partner on one side, the dog on the other, the baby on your chest, all snoring, all dreaming.

Every day you read to the baby. Too young to understand the words or see the pictures properly, you know, but you think the baby likes to hear your voice. You start with poems that are fun to read aloud: Alfred Noyes' 'The Highwayman', Edgar Allan Poe's 'The Raven', T. S. Eliot's 'The Love Song of J. Alfred Prufrock', which is a poem your dad used to read aloud to you when you were little and wouldn't sleep; you remember your rabbit-print wallpaper blurry in the dusk, his drowsy weight beside you on the bed, his day-worn voice intoning the lines. Then you just read aloud to the baby whatever book you're reading: a memoir of insomnia, a horror poetry collection, an Icelandic thriller, some classic ghost stories. But your partner walks in on you reading the baby a graphic description of a horror film in which a woman is buried alive. You protest that the baby can't understand, but you stop anyway. She brings you a stack of picture books.

You're sent the audio files of the novel you finished while pregnant. You couldn't go to London to be present for the full-cast recording of the novel, as it happened the exact week you gave birth. The producer sent you updates, photos of the cast doing thumbs-up in the recording studio, and you liked that; it made you feel like things were happening. Sure, you were bleeding and terrified and obsessed with your own nipples, but look, you're still a writer. You listen to the audio files, all ten hours of them, while looking after the baby. You think about wearing headphones but that feels worse somehow, as if you're intentionally blocking out the baby. The novel contains death and sex and toxic masculinity and lots of instances of the word fuck. *The baby can't understand*, you tell yourself, turning the volume down.

Your favourite picture books to read the baby are about night. Perhaps this is the case for all new parents, as there are plenty of them. Night feels different with a baby. You've slept through so much of the night without ever knowing it. But now you know it. Reluctantly, but still. Before, sleep was a ritual: it had to be called up with certain scents (lavender essential oil on the pillow), certain textures (memory foam pillow), certain sounds (plane crash podcast), certain amounts of light (none). Now you're asleep the moment your eyes close. It's a new kind of tiredness. One you feel in your bones. One that pulls you down, like sinking to the bottom of a pool. One that waits for you, one that welcomes you, heavy as velvet.

People say of the newborn stage: don't worry, it doesn't last long.

People also say: enjoy it, it doesn't last long.

When the baby is two weeks old, you stop bleeding. You start dreaming. You didn't even realise, until it starts again, that you'd stopped.

The baby starts laughing. Mostly while asleep. Juddering chuckles in the back of the throat. You didn't realise, before having a baby, how noisy babies are. You didn't know much at all about babies. You'd never been left alone with one, not before your own exited your body and was handed to you. You knew about crying and burbling baby talk, but it's more than that. The baby grunts, coos, sighs, squeaks, sneezes, trills, huffs, whistles. You do your best to listen; to learn this new language.

5

There's the time your mother-in-law is holding the baby, and the baby is wailing, and you have a feeling that a nappy change is needed even though you did one just a minute ago, and your mother-in-law is rocking the baby because she thinks a bit of rocking is needed, and you want her to give you the baby because you can't bear the sounds of distress, but you wait anxiously, standing too close to her, stroking the baby's head, wanting her to pass you the baby, and tentatively you say, *I'll take the baby*, and your mother-in-law, wanting to give you a break, wanting to do her part as a member of your village, says, *It's okay*, and steps back with the baby in her arms, and you nod and smile and go into the bedroom cupboard, which is the furthest-away place without leaving the house, and you cry, and you tell your partner you're only crying because the baby is crying but it's because you know, you just know, that the baby needs you, specifically and only you, but you can't say that because that would be insulting to the baby's other mother and to your mother-in-law, who also love the baby, who love the baby just as much as you do, and who know just as much about mothering as you do. But you want the baby. You want silence and space and time and not to be touched and not to have to change nappies and not to have to walk around the room joggling a small screeching thing but at the same time you want the baby, you want the baby, you need the baby, give me the fucking baby right now.

There's the morning that your partner sleeps in and you potter around the flat with the sleeping baby in a sling, unloading the dishwasher, replying to emails, sorting the laundry. You make yourself a black-and-white breakfast (black coffee, boiled eggs, blueberries and yogurt) and, when the baby yells awake, you read out the contract for this book as a lullaby. You feel like a power mum from an 80s movie. Like you're holding the world in your arms. Your mind is clear and everything is under control.

Then there's the evening your mum babysits and you and your partner go out for dinner. You're still upset about not breastfeeding, but on the plus side you get to have your first glass of wine in a year. The time with your partner is great.

The food is great. The wine is great. The wine is fucking transcendent.

But –

Mum has a metal plate in her wrist, you say to your partner. *What if something goes wrong with her wrist, and she drops the baby?*

Mum says she had a bad sleep last night, you say to your partner. *What if she falls asleep with the baby on her chest and the baby rolls off and lands with a bang on the floor?*

Mum breastfed me and my brother so she's never made formula milk before, you say to your partner. *What if she does the bottle wrong and scalds the baby's mouth?*

Mum said she plans to take the baby for a walk in the pram, you say to your partner. *What if a bad driver mounts the kerb and ploughs into the pram? What if there's a bee that stings the baby, a spider that bites the baby, a fly that flies into the baby's mouth, a rabid dog that bites the baby?*

There aren't any rabid dogs in this country, your partner says, and gently takes your hand. *Would you like me to text your mum to watch out for rabid dogs?* You consider. *No,* you say, and top up your wine.

There's the time that you take the baby out to brunch with your friend, and the café is long and thin, and there's nowhere to put the pram, so you tuck it into the side as best you can, and every few minutes people try to get past and you push at the pram, not moving it at all. You almost want someone to say. *You're not even trying to move it*, so you can say, *You know what? I'm fucking not trying and why should I? It's not my fault this café only suits thin people who don't have prams or wheelchairs or a body any wider than a 30cm school ruler.* But to your disappointment, no one says anything. You realise that you never cared before about where prams could go, out in the world. Now you care with an indignant rage. But you know that as soon as the baby doesn't need a pram, you won't care again.

There's the time that your partner's stepfather texts to ask if he can pop over, because he hasn't been round in a few days and misses the baby. You sit on the couch, sipping a cup of tea, and watch him walk circles around your front room with the baby resting on his shoulder. You think about how before the baby was born, everyone in your family was very excited, and no one seemed to care who was or wasn't biologically related to the baby. But still you worried. Everyone spoke about the baby as if it was theirs, but would they really feel it? Or were they just saying what they know they should? Now you realise that was just another thing you didn't need to worry about.

There's the time, soon after your partner has gone back to work, that you and the baby go for a walk in the park together, and you realise what being alone with the baby reminds you of. It's like a writing residency. You used to go once or twice a year, for a month at a time, to Finland or Iceland or Spain or Sweden or other places in Scotland. On residency, your entire focus is on the book you're writing. The book defines when you sleep (when you can't write any more), when you eat (when you can't write any more), when you read or go out for a walk or call a friend to weep about how you're a hack and you'll never write again. Now the baby defines your patterns. You're familiar with this. The single-mindedness. The living outside of everyday routine. The focus on quiet and small tasks. The sense of a slow building, piece by piece, to grow something magical.

There's the time that your partner goes out and you and the baby sit on the couch and the baby cuddles into you. Not sleeping, just holding you. The baby holds onto you like a koala to a tree. Like a sailor to a ship's mast in a storm. You know that soon the baby will sleep, safe there cuddled into you. You could also sleep. You could read. You could write something. You could reply to some emails. You could make plans for stories you want to write, places you want to visit, people you want to meet up with. You could do all of these things without moving. But you choose nothing. You choose the beauty of absolutely nothing. Because it's not nothing. It's oxytocin release, it's slowing both your heart-beats, it's strengthening your bond, it's lowering stress, it's helping your uterus to go back to its pre-pregnancy state, it's doing several other things that you will google later, but you don't google them right now, you just sit with the baby holding you, and you simply exist.

There's the time that you and your partner and the baby and your donor all go for a walk together. Standing on the corner of your street, your donor holds the baby while your partner adjusts the straps of the baby carrier you're wearing. A passing man cheerfully asks how old the baby is, and congratulates your donor on his beautiful family. You're not sure how your partner fits into this imagined family: your sister who looks nothing like you, maybe. A cousin. A passer-by who's just very good at adjusting baby carriers. You chat to the passing man for a bit; your donor, clearly uncomfortable, says: *It's their baby; they're the mums.* You, equally uncomfortable, add: *He's a friend. An uncle!* When the passing man continues passing, your donor says, *I guess he thought I was the dad.* Which he is. And isn't.

You all walk together through the necropolis and you try not to cry at all the graves for babies; one grave in particu-lar haunts you: a man who lost all five children before the age of five, then his wife, then lived on for another twenty years. That same day, it starts to smirr with rain and you hold your hands over the baby's head to keep it dry; you can't stop looking at that little face, the damp eyelashes sparkling, the tiny tongue peeking out to taste the unfamiliar rain.

You notice that whenever something happens – the rain starts, a cute dog crosses your path, a siren sounds in the distance – you don't look at it. You look instead at the baby's reaction.

That same day you all see a double rainbow and decide it's a blessing on your big queer family.

6

One afternoon, the baby falls asleep on your chest. You press your hands to the baby's back, holding your bodies close. Those shoulder blades like little wings. The dimple where the tail should be. That skin, poreless and translucent, newly peeled from the months underwater, the temples blue-veined, the chin a swipe of porcelain. The eyes the colour of deep water. This is the sort of baby that would be stolen by a goblin king. You know the baby's body better than you know your own. You lean in and let your breathing slow, inhaling each exhaled breath. Your tiny animal. Your familiar. Your heart, pulled out of your body.

Your partner gets Covid. She's angry and upset about this, as you both managed to get two years through the pandemic without getting it. She refers to it as 'Covid-19', like a parent using a child's full name to scold it. She sleeps on the couch, wears a mask at all times, and sits by the open window even though it's winter. She doesn't touch you or the baby for a full week until she tests negative, and you think it's worked, aren't you clever, no pandemic for you, but then you and the baby both test positive. Every newspaper image of Covid death flashes in your mind. You're instantly terrified that you'll die, probably tomorrow, on a ventilator, and you won't see the baby grow up, and the baby won't remember you, and you'll be nothing more than a ghost, a story, something that only existed in theory. You used to, in idle teenage moments, morbidly revel in images of your own death: how sad everyone would be, what a loss of potential, so young. Now the concept of your death fills you with rage.

You think of your labour, the baby caught and twisted, trying to push through, shoulders turned like a man in a stiff breeze on a winter beach, trying to get out into the world even though it's hopeless. You see that determination already, in the way the baby will try to sit up or reach out for a toy, never getting frustrated but patiently trying again, again, again. You want to do that for the baby. You want to keep trying. You did keep trying, you and your partner both, and if the two of you can pass anything on you want it to be that. Try, baby. Keep trying.

Midway through your Covid isolation, you are not in a good mood. You are exhausted and moody. The baby woke at 3 a.m. and 6 a.m. and wouldn't be soothed until you went and made a bottle; your partner fed the baby the bottle, but it didn't matter; you were awake by then, and lay in the dark, wondering if you could hear a rattle in your chest. To distract yourself from your inevitable demise, you look at social media. The first thing you see is a photo of an acquaintance who had a baby a month after you. She's on holiday somewhere sunny. She has a flat stomach and perfect skin. She doesn't look exhausted or like she's contemplating her own inevitable demise. How is that possible? How is she handling this so much better than you? Why don't you look like that? You put your phone down and go into the bathroom and cry, running the tap because you don't want your partner to hear and comfort you. Later you retrieve your phone. The photo is still up on the screen. You notice what you didn't notice before: the photo was taken six years ago. You have been comparing yourself to a ghost.

You don't die of Covid, and neither does the baby. You're vaccinated, and barely even feel ill. You got your first vaccination while pregnant, and even though you were told the immunity wouldn't pass to the baby, you still hope it did. After a week, you both test negative.

The baby has learned to grab. The baby grabs a cup of tea and spills it on the carpet. The baby grabs a magazine and rips off the cover. The baby grabs your hair and yanks it. You google: *How to tell baby loves me.*

The first thing the baby ever did is shit in you. The doctor told you this when you woke from your C-section surgery. They lifted the baby from your body, and right away, just like that: shat inside you, into the cavity of your organs. The creature that you love more than anything in the world literally shat in you. And the only love comparable to your love for the baby is the baby's love for you.

You watch a video about C-section scar massage. None of the midwives or health visitors has ever mentioned this; once the wound has closed, as far as anyone is concerned, it's finished: just put your clothes on and don't think about it. Your days of being concerned about how you look in a bikini are gone; were gone even before you were pregnant. But still, you think anything you can do to help yourself heal is surely good. You want to get your body back. Not in the way it's meant in the flyers in the gym that make you feel shit about yourself. Not getting it back to the way it was before. But getting it back as in retrieving it. As in reclaiming for yourself something which was taken.

You run a hot bath and get the oil. You think, like you thought about the perineal massage, that this could be a sexy time. Medical; but sexy. You make a playlist of tongue-in-cheek sexy songs. 'I Wanna Sex You Up'. 'I'll Make Love to You'. 'Sexual Healing'. You start massaging your scar just like in the video. The woman in the video has a flat stomach and her scar is thin and silvery. You have to flatten your stomach with your palms before you can see your scar. It's not as wide as you thought it would be; you don't see how a whole entire baby came out of there. One end of it is thin and pale, the other thicker, pinker. That's the part where they tied off the stitches. You start massaging. It feels lumpy underneath. Your skin moves oddly. You think of a scalpel. You think of yourself, unconscious, tubes in your mouth, tubes in your arms, lying flat on a table under bright lights, surrounded by strangers, your organs pulled outside your body. Your body and all the things that were done to it. Your body, there without you. Your partner comes into the bathroom to find you cradling your belly, sobbing to 'Sexual Healing'.

Let me help, she says, and she gets you out of the bath and dries you off and lies you down and gently, gently, she massages your scar. She doesn't say it's okay. She doesn't say not to cry. She doesn't say to just not look at it. She doesn't say it will go away, because she knows it won't, and that you don't want it to anyway.

Your body is a stranger to you now. You think about all the things it's done and all the things you've done with it, to it. All the things you've asked of it and expected of it. You've used it reluctantly and joyously, without thinking and after years of planning. You've used it to make money, to cause pain, to give and receive pleasure. As display, as function, as proof. Now you've used it to make another body inside itself. Now it's healing, resettling, reshaping itself – not into the same shape it occupied before, but something new again.

You pore over photos of celebrity mothers. They are thin. Their bellies are flat. They look like they never gave birth. You feel like your body, to have any kind of value, should also look like it never gave birth. You know this is ridiculous. That's what you chose to use it for, and you're not trying to hide the fact.

You and your partner take the baby swimming. Your dad took you swimming every week from when you were a month old, and you love the water. You want the baby to love it too. You bypass the outdoor pool, with its scattering leaves and rain and enormous sky, and head instead for the baby pool, which is knee-deep and as warm as a bath. You watch your partner sway the baby through the water, singing songs, splashing the tiny tufty head. The baby's hands hold tight to your partner's shoulders. You didn't want to wear your maternity swimsuit so you've bought a new one: a bikini, made of two triangles that do not disguise the sag of your post-milk breasts, and bottoms that do not cover the bulge of your post-baby belly. You stand in the water, proud. This body made a life. Why should you hide it? Why the fuck should you hide it?

You don't care. Then you do. Then you don't care. Then you do. You don't know your body, and you don't know how to feel about it.

Your partner has taken the baby out and you're alone. You stand in front of the bathroom mirror and look at your body. You don't find it easy. You don't recognise the person in the mirror as yourself. You see unpainted toenails and swollen feet. You see unshaven calves and thighs topped with the uneven pinkish dashes of stretch marks, the skin puckering around them. You see stretch marks also on the hips, the belly, the breasts. The breasts sag, the nipples not tilting up but shrugging off to the sides. The nipples are still the purple they darkened to in pregnancy, the colour of a next-day bruise. The belly button is deep and uneven, big enough to swallow a fingertip to the first knuckle. The backside crinkles. The back folds. The arms are dry and blotchy. The face – you can't even look. You know you should be proud of this body. You should celebrate

what it's achieved and find it beautiful. You'll get there.
You think, you hope. You'll get to know this person. But
not yet. You put the shower on hot so that the mirror
steams over.

7

The baby is six months old and you are writing a book. It's called *The Unfamiliar* because that's how your body has been made, how your life has been made. Unfamiliar, as in something you don't recognise. But also, a witch's familiar, a tiny creature that goes on a journey with you, a source of power who you can't communicate with through language. But mostly, a family.

So, you imagine being asked, *how DO you write a book with a baby?* You imagine the Q&A session at a literary festival, the posh upmarket sort that always make you feel incredibly uncomfortable but also have the best food and opportunities for celebrity-spotting in the green room. You imagine yourself smiling wryly as you answer: *Well, there's a reason the book is in small chunks.* You imagine yourself explaining that that's how you think now, with a baby: in chunks.

Also, you imagine yourself adding, it helps the writing that you no longer have the time or energy for certain things. Digital self-harm. Getting angry at strangers' tweets. Comparing yourself to other mothers' Instagram photos. Social media in general. One of the contradictions in being a writer that you've never quite squared is the desire for everyone to look at you and listen to you, and also to crawl into a cave and hide. Soon after the baby was born, something you'd written was published, and you didn't have the time or energy to pay attention to the sound of it being received; and then a little later, you checked and realised there wasn't much of a sound at all. The book, which took you a year to write, seemed to have dropped into an abyss, falling fast into deep black water. You felt a lingering disappointment, but at the same time you realised you liked the quiet. You'd long had a fantasy of a little attic room with nothing in it but a laptop and a notebook, a desk and a chair; of spending all your time writing and then posting the pages under the door to some strange person on the other side and you'd never have to think about what they did with them.

Also, you imagine yourself continuing, and you're really getting into the swing of it now, waffling on about your books and your life and many other topics that frankly you had no business opining on, also you like that your life is smaller now, simpler. You don't read books you're not enjoying. You don't give your time to people who don't deserve it. You don't do anything that doesn't need to be done. You cleared your Netflix queue, deleted your Books to Read list, gave away all the DVDs you'd been hoarding and still claimed you were going to watch even though years had gone by without you watching them. You love, now, the joy of things abandoned, things discarded.

So when it comes to writing with a baby, you imagine yourself saying, it's actually fine, it's better than you thought it would be, because—

But you stop. You stop imaging yourself sipping wine and smiling wryly and talking about your small-chunk book and allowing people to imagine you as a super-mum, a super-writer, casually setting down your smiling and well-rested baby to quietly play with an organic hand-painted abacus while you tap out another chunk. Because that's dishonest.

You try to write with the baby there. It doesn't go very well. You stop writing the bit about going to a book festival in Malaysia to wrestle the baby into little moon-print dungarees. You stop writing the bit about the perineal

massage to take away the crocheted giraffe rattle that the
baby is getting annoyed at and replace it with a wooden
ball with jangly—

That's a bit that you try to write, again, with the baby there,
and that's all that's in your notes, they stop mid-sentence
and you can't remember the point that you were going to
make. You think what you wanted to say is that you hav-
en't, at all, figured out how to write with the baby.

You actually write much of this book, or the notes for
the book at least, in the years before you're pregnant, and
during your pregnancy, particularly in the two weeks when
the baby is overdue, when you're desperate to be doing
something so you don't obsess over the baby dying. Then
you write notes on your phone in the hospital soon after the
birth when you can't sleep, and using voice-to-text when
you think of sentences in your head while walking round
the flat joggling the baby to sleep, and during night feeds
when the baby has drifted off.

But still, that's only notes, not the actual book. At three
months old, your mum and mother-in-law take the baby
three days a week between them so that you can work;
though you still don't write the book then, as you have
to catch up on all the work you missed during the three
months you and your partner were both on maternity leave,

and to make some money to buy very small socks and nappies and milk and a dozen plastic devices and gadgets that are now vital even though you'd never even heard of them before having a baby. The real writing happens when the baby is six months old, when you go on a week-long writing residency and sit in a chair for an entire week and write for twelve hours a day, stopping only to sleep or eat. You write with a speed and intensity you've never had before. So you don't, actually, write a book with a baby. That's how you do it.

You miss being pregnant. You miss having a newborn. You say to your partner and family and friends how much you loved being pregnant, and although they don't argue with you, they look at you for a second too long before replying.

When you look back over your notes for this book, you realise why everyone left a pause when you said you loved being pregnant. You spent the entire time terrified that the baby would die. You did enjoy it – parts of it – but on balance, you spent much of it afraid. You're glad that you made so many notes, so that you could write the book in the moment, in the emotion. The advice on writing memoir is that it needs time, space; that you need to have distance from what happened, so that you can make sense of it all. You don't disagree, but also you're glad you didn't give yourself space. If you'd written it all later, looking back and trying to remember, you'd play it down. You'd make fun of yourself for being anxious. You'd play up your fears of death, your own and the baby's, because it would be funny, because you didn't die. But why do you think you have to pretend that you weren't afraid? That you're not still afraid?

You paste the phrase 'you're going to miscarry anyway so it's all for nothing' into the book notes on your laptop, because it's a repeated phrase in part of the book so you want to make sure you phrase it the same each time. Then you delete the phrase. It looks too stark like that. It looks like it's temping fate. The baby is born, the baby is six months old, the baby is perfectly healthy. And still, the fear of miscarriage is so great that it doesn't go away just because it can't happen. It lingers, it stains, it ghosts, the fear.

8

A few years ago, when you were halfway through writing a book of horror stories, you had a fight with your partner. It was over something stupid and you made up fast, but during the argument, even as you were thinking of things you could drag up from the past few months, fading barbs that you could use to win the argument, to show that you weren't the only shitty one around here, you thought: Use this. Use this feeling.

For what? For a story. You didn't want to write a story for money (or not only for money) or for attention (or not only for attention) or for prestige (or not only for prestige). You wanted to write it for something else. Truth, maybe. To make it seem worth it.

So you wrote a story about a character who makes parts of their body into tiny houses to gift to their partner, but each thing they give (a tooth, an ear, a tongue) is insufficient, until finally they make a house of their entire body, knowing that that, still, can never be enough, because that's how you felt in that moment, arguing with your partner.

And now you think: maybe you are the only shitty one around here. Because it was something real, and you made it a story, and you tell yourself (and others, strangers and acquaintances and friends, into a microphone, on stage at some book festival) that making it into a story was noble. You used your truth nobly; you put your own feelings aside and held your noble head high and made it into a story, a neat little thing that other people could read and perhaps be comforted or challenged or surprised by. So truthful. So noble. But is that really what you did? Is that really why you did it? And then, a year later, when you'd finished that book, and started another one, your partner miscarried. She miscarried again. You couldn't get pregnant, and then you could. Your baby almost died during birth. And each time you thought: Use this. Use this.

Well, here it is. You're using it.

You're writing a story of being the other mother, a story of miscarriages and failed IVF, a story of coming to the end of the road on the journey to become a parent. But it's also a story of an easy conception, an easy pregnancy, and an easy baby. Both of these apparently contradictory stories happening to the same two people.

You worry about being accused of navel gazing. Well, look at your navel. Look at it. The leering grin of your belly button. The stretch marks, already faded silvery. An entire human life grew in your navel. Why shouldn't you look at it? Why shouldn't you write from it?

Your partner takes the baby out for a walk, and bumps into an acquaintance you haven't seen in a while. He asks: *So how did you manage to have a baby, since you're both women?* She replies: *That's quite a personal question, and I'd rather not answer.*

Weeks later, you're out with the baby and you bump into the same acquaintance; you chitchat and mention you're writing a book about queer pregnancy and parenthood. *I bumped into your partner recently,* he says, *and I asked how exactly you'd had the baby, and she said it was personal.* You nod, as you already know this, as your partner already told you. *So,* he says, *how did you have the baby? Did you carry, or did she?* You, not sure whether to be offended or amused, say: *Well, as my partner told you, it's personal.* He looks confused. *But you're writing a book about it,* he says. *So how can it be?*

When you were writing that book of horror stories, there was one story that you tried to write multiple times, but always abandoned. You never finished it. You wanted to write about a dream you had, about staying in a house with a door that wouldn't stay closed. You'd close and lock the door, but then you'd hear the sound of a person in the next room and realise someone was in the house, and you'd see that the door was, somehow, wide open. The real fear underlying it was about lack of control. The real fear was that if you open the door a little bit – by writing a book about yourself and your family, say – it can then get shoved open all the way; that someone can come inside.

You're writing a whole book in the second person because you couldn't bring yourself to say 'I'.

Your heart is bruised now. Your skin is raw, a graze stinging in the cold air. You cry at documentaries, news reports, songs. Even things that you know are cynically engineered specifically to make you cry – you know it, but you still cry. You haven't helped that feeling by writing this book. Every minute of working on it has felt like staring at yourself in an extra-strength magnifying mirror. Every wrinkle, every scar. The slight swell of your eyelid where you seem to be getting an eye infection again. The hateful way your cheek bulges at the corner of your mouth, jowly. But also, the bright blue of your eyes. Your soppy smile when you think about your partner and the baby. So you get out the mirror, and you look at yourself; and then you ignore it all, and go inside yourself, into the dark heartbeat depths; and you write.

You're doing the final edits on this book. The baby is almost one; toddling around the room like a drunk zombie; eating pasta and bananas and blueberries and, just like in very earliest life, potato; saying *dog* and *Mama* and *Mum*.

All you want to do now is to hold the book and the baby out to the world, tentative and boastful, and say: *Look what I made. It took ages, and it hurt, and I loved it, and I would do it again, even knowing all this, even knowing everything.*

Thank you

Books and babies take a village. Here is mine.

Anbara S / Bernie C / Camilla G / Cathryn S / Daisy J / David B / Francine T / Granny E / Granny J / Grandpa G / Grandpa R / Hannah K / Heather P x2 / Imogen HG / Jac C / Jen C / Jessie B / Lily B / Lizzie M / Nell S / Rachelle A / Rose T / Rosie BL / Sheena C / Sophie C / Susie B / Susie F / Nonno.

And Annie, always.

Acknowledgements

Part of this book originally commissioned by Canary Wharf Arts + Events for the 'Short Story Stations: Pride Takeover' as part of Pride at Canary Wharf.

Part of this book originally published in *Counterpoint* magazine.

Thank you to Cove Park residency (particularly Alexia and Alex), where this book was edited.

At Little, Brown: Niamh Anderson, Zoe Carroll, Lilly Cox, Marie Hrynczak, Anna Kelly, Cassandra Rigg, Ellen Rockell, Matilda Singer and Alison Tulett.